In Pursuit of Kindness

by Jason Farley

*Whoever pursues righteousness and kindness
will find life, righteousness, and honor.*
—Prov. 21:21

www.jovial-pub.com

Copyright © 2019 Jason Farley
All rights reserved. This book or any portion thereof may not be reproduced or used in any manner whatsoever without the express written permission of the publisher except for the use of brief quotations in a book review.

Printed in the United States of America

ISBN: 978-0-9998050-3-9

Second Edition
First Printing, 2019

All Scripture quotations, unless otherwise noted, are from the *ESV® Bible* (*The Holy Bible, English Standard Version®*), copyright © 2001 by Crossway Bibles, a publishing ministry of Good News Publishers. Used by permission. All rights reserved.

Jovial Publishers
2106 E. 63rd Ave
Spokane, WA 99223

www.jovial-pub.com

IN PURSUIT OF KINDNESS

Jason Farley

To my Mom, who is the kindest person I know.

Preface

I am not naturally a kind person. I am tempted constantly and consistently to cynicism. In fact, when I walked myself through the doors of a church, I had spent the previous night watching *Saturday Night Live* and listening to the eminently misanthropic joke punk band *The Dead Milkmen*. One of my favorite songs was 'If *You Love Someone Set Them on Fire.*' And that was pretty much my take on kindness when I first showed up at First Presbyterian Church in downtown Spokane.

But God, who is rich in mercy, has led me like a rail-riding hobo. I was suspicious of any kindness, convinced that there always had to be a self-serving agenda. God has been patient with me because, quite frankly, he is kind.

This, for me, has probably been the single-most surprising of God's traits. Completely unexpected. I was not looking for a kind God. Kindness seemed neither particularly important nor divine.

I was convinced that the truth about life, God, and the world would be like medicine. It would taste bad but be good for you. Any sweetness was, at best, an illusion, and at worst a downright lie.

But I kept running up against an indisputable fact. In the history of God's people, the lovingkindness of God has been the defining feature of our story. I found myself to have been grafted into a history of God's surprising kindness. At least, it was surprising to me. This book is me coming to terms with God's kindness, what it means to follow a kind God, and what it means to be in pursuit of kindness.

Contents

i	Preface
1	Introduction
7	Two Kinds of Kings
19	Kind Like God
41	Words that Build
57	Get Rid of All Bitterness
69	Parenting with Kindness
87	Receivers Give
97	Legal Hatred
113	When I Don't Want to be Kind
125	Kindness by Faith
137	Joseph the Shame-bearer
151	Covered in Fig Leaves

Introduction

When I was a young Christian, I visited a church that was having an evening service. I was filling in on the drums. I had never been to a service at this church, but when I came in the front door there were two small gray-haired ladies sitting in rocking chairs in the foyer.

I was there with my friend who had grown up in the church, so even though I was a visitor, I was obviously someone who was supposed to be there. Behind us, though, a jaded looking punk rock kid walked in. He wore a 16" mohawk above a severe expression. His hair was preschool primary-color blue and stood straight up off the center of his skull. From the back of his head to the middle of his forehead he was fully committed to this mohawk. It took time, effort, and probably a dozen eggs to accomplish such an impressive feat of engineering. He looked like he was in the wrong room and was about to realize that he had accidentally wandered into a church.

These two little old ladies got up and started walking towards him and I thought, 'Oh No. Here it comes.' I figured they were going to let him know that he was in the wrong spot and send him on his way. But then one of the ladies said, "Hi there, I just have to ask, How do you make it do that? That is amazing!"

The kid explained, a little defensively about egg whites and hair dye and the other lady said, "Can I touch it?"

He smiled and tilted his head forward and both of the ladies giggle as they poked his hair. Then they each gave him a big hug. He looked a little stunned as they each took an arm so that he could escort them into the service. They wanted to make sure to sit with him.

I guarantee that kid did not expect that. When he decided to give himself a shockingly blue mohawk before he came to church he was probably after a response from the little old ladies. But the kindness of these two wonderful little grandmothers was not the reaction that he expected.

That is the way that the kindness that God has shown us should manifest itself. When we are in the grip of God's kindness to us, we will look for ways to be God's outstretched arms to whoever God puts in front of us.

Christians should be kind. God has been kind to each of us after all. The church that knows how to be kind to sinners is the church that remembers. The church is sinners that have received God's kindness. Kindness should mark the church. True kindness, the sort that envelops sinners with God's forgiveness, that embraces, and loves, and helps, and lifts up, should mark the way that the people of God treat one another, and the way that we interact with the world.

But often, though we want to quit being harsh and selfish, we are never quite able to get a handle on what we are supposed to be replacing our malevolence with. That is what this book is about. You can never put off the old man without putting on the new man. You will never put off unkindness without putting on kindness. And to follow Christ, we should be in pursuit of kindness.

"Whoever pursues righteousness and kindness will find life, righteousness, and honor" (Proverbs 21:21).

There are three things that you will find when pursuing kindness: life, righteousness, and honor. True life is found in the pursuit of kindness and righteousness. Righteousness means doing what is right. The people in the world that are most alive are those that are doing what is right and are kind to whomever is in front of them. Though we sing that nice guys finish last, Solomon teaches us that those that are pursuing kindness will have people do right by them. Those that put others first with kindness will find that honor flows in their direction.

This is not the only place where we are told that God calls us to be kind. The prophet Micah sums up the call of God on all of the descendants of Adam. *"He has told you, O man, what is good; and what does the Lord require of you but to do justice, and to love kindness, and to walk humbly with your God?"* (Micah 6:8). Again, doing what is right and kindness are summary statements of what it is to follow God.

Kindness, coupled with righteousness, is the way we walk after God. Kindness in pursuit of doing right leads to life, righteousness, and honor. God says that the call on the life of every person is to do justice, love kindness, and to walk humbly with our God. And so we must pursue of kindness.

But to do that, we must first understand what kindness is.

Two Kinds of Kings

Jesus fed 5000 men, plus women and children, using only five loaves and two fish. It is one of the more famous of Jesus' miracles. An enormous crowd was following Jesus through the wilderness like Moses leading the multitudes out of Egypt. The people are hungry just like the multitudes with Moses. And just like the Israelites following Moses, miraculous wilderness food shows up.

There is another unexpected meal in Matthew's Gospel. Herod had taken his brother's wife and children. He made a show of marrying her., but it merely made his evil legal. John the baptizer preached that Herod had sinned by illegally taking his brother's wife.

Herod had John arrested.

But because John was popular with the people, Herod had not actually done anything with his prisoner. He was too scared to upset the mob. While John was waiting in prison, Herod's new wife was busily conspiring with his niece/step-daughter to trick Herod into executing John.

When Herod threw a party for the rich and powerful in Jerusalem, his step-daughter is a part of the entertainment. She dances excellently and the guests are so happy with her that Herod makes a foolish vow, "Whatever you want, up to half of his kingdom." (Of course, the kingdom is not actually his, since he is only ruling at the pleasure of the Roman Emperor).

She asks for John's head on a plate.

Herod consistently acts out of fear. He has had

John waiting in prison because he fears the crowds. He fears a loss of face before the wealthy more. He knows it is a bad idea, but he has John executed and his head put out on a serving platter with the rest of the dinner.

These two scenes of leaders providing unexpected food are both generally well-known stories. But what is often missed is the fact that Matthew tells them together. Telling them side-by-side contrasts visions that these two rulers have for their kingdoms. Herod is a king that eats his people. Jesus is a king that feeds his people.

> *At that time Herod the tetrarch heard about the fame of Jesus, and he said to his servants, "This is John the Baptist. He has been raised from the dead; that is why these miraculous powers are at work in him." For Herod had seized John and bound him and put him in prison for the sake of Herodias, his brother Philip's wife, because John had been saying to him, "It is not lawful for you to have her." And though he wanted to put him to death, he feared the people, because they held him to be a prophet. But when Herod's birthday came, the daughter of Herodias danced before the company and pleased Herod,*

so that he promised with an oath to give her whatever she might ask. Prompted by her mother, she said, "Give me the head of John the Baptist here on a platter." And the king was sorry, but because of his oaths and his guests he commanded it to be given. He sent and had John beheaded in the prison, and his head was brought on a platter and given to the girl, and she brought it to her mother.

And his disciples came and took the body and buried it, and they went and told Jesus. Now when Jesus heard this, he withdrew from there in a boat to a desolate place by himself. But when the crowds heard it, they followed him on foot from the towns. When he went ashore he saw a great crowd, and he had compassion on them and healed their sick. Now when it was evening, the disciples came to him and said, "This is a desolate place, and the day is now over; send the crowds away to go into the villages and buy food for themselves." But Jesus said, "They need not go away; you give them something to eat." They said to him, "We have only five loaves here and two fish." And he said, "Bring them here to me." Then he ordered the crowds to sit down on the grass, and taking the five loaves and the two fish, he looked up to heaven and said a blessing. Then he broke the loaves and gave them to the disciples, and the disciples gave them to the crowds. And they all ate and were satisfied. And they took up twelve baskets full of the broken pieces left over. And those who ate were about five thousand men, besides women and children (Matthew 14:1–21).

Two kinds of kings. Two kinds of kingdoms. The first kingdom is a devouring kingdom. And God's people are on the menu. The king eats the people and following his lead the citizens feed on one another.

But in the kingdom of God, King Jesus feeds his people. He has compassion and makes sure that people are fed. He brings his disciples in to help him feed the crowds. His kingdom is to be a kingdom where the citizens feed one another rather than eat one another.

A king can be judged by the laws he makes. When Paul turns to explain the sum and substance of the law of God, he explains that God's law keeps us from eating one another.

> *For the whole law is fulfilled in one word: "You shall love your neighbor as yourself." But if you bite and devour one another, watch out that you are not consumed by one another* (Galatians 5:14–15).

The citizen's of Jesus' Kingdom should not bite and devour one another. Instead, we love our neighbors as ourselves.

Kingdoms like Herod's kingdom are ruled by fear instead of love. Fear subjects people to the old ways of the flesh. In fear-founded kingdoms people are consumables. Paul explains what it looks like when we eat one another.

> *Now the works of the flesh are evident: sexual immorality, impurity, sensuality, idolatry, sorcery, enmity, strife, jealousy, fits of anger, rivalries, dissensions, divisions, envy, drunkenness, orgies, and things like these. I warn you, as I warned you before, that those who do such things will not inherit the kingdom of God* (Galatians 5:19–21).

These are each selfish ways of dealing with the people in our lives. They are all ways in which we bite and devour our neighbor rather than following Jesus and feeding one another. These are not what it looks like to be a citizen of the king that fed the 5000.

Instead, we are supposed to be like Jesus and feed

one another.

> *But the fruit of the Spirit is love, joy, peace, patience, kindness, goodness, faithfulness, gentleness, self-control; against such things there is no law* (Galatians 5:22–23).

What do you do with fruit? You eat it. Or in this case, you feed one another with it. And notice what Paul says, "Against such, there is no law." None of these things are illegal. The King has not forbidden any of these things.

Paul is explaining life as a citizen in the kingdom of Jesus. We do not devour one another; we feed one another. And we feed one another on the fruit of the Spirit. As God grows fruit in our lives, it is so that we can feed one another, build one another up, and give our fruit to one another.

We do not use one another, or treat each other as expendable commodities. Instead we treat one another as people to love, enjoy, be at peace with, be patient with, show kindness towards, be good to, keep faith with, and control ourselves for. As we feed one another on the fruit of the Spirit, we discover why the kingdom of God cannot be moved. It is built on a solid foundation of love, not on the wobbly foundation of fear. Therefore, Jesus' kingdom is not going anywhere. It will neither be conquered nor destroy itself.

But often the church acts like frogs eating dragonflies. Frogs eat dragonflies live, snagging them right out of the air. When dragonfly larvae transform in the early spring they fill the air thick. Frogs have been known to greedily fill their mouths so full of living dragonflies that they are unable to close their jaw.

It quits being about satisfying hunger. Their mouths will be too full even to swallow. They snag and snatch dragonflies out of the insect fog until their jowl is locked open on their living prey. It is not about fulfilling needs. They continue to jam and cram more and more dragonflies into their mouth until they are incapacitated. The only thing that stops them from biting and devouring is limited space between their lips.

Our flesh will tell itself that it is only taking what is ours by right. Our flesh will tell us that we only nibble what we need. But we need nothing won by the works of the flesh. We gain nothing in consuming our neighbor. Resist the impulse to bite, devour, and use people.

It is not that we are not in need. It is only that our neighbor will not provide what we need. Instead, we should follow Jesus, who offers Himself as food for us.

> *Truly, truly, I say to you, whoever believes has eternal life. I am the bread of life. Your fathers ate the manna in the wilderness, and they died. This is the bread that comes down from heaven, so that one may eat of it and not die. I am the living bread that came down from heaven. If anyone eats of this bread, he will live forever. And the bread that I will give for the life of the world is my flesh." The Jews then disputed among themselves, saying, "How can this man give us his flesh to eat?" So Jesus said to them, "Truly, truly, I say to you, unless you eat the flesh of the Son of Man and drink his blood, you have no life in you. Whoever feeds on my flesh and drinks my blood has eternal life, and I will raise him up on the last day. For my flesh is true food, and my blood is true drink. Whoever feeds on my flesh and drinks my blood abides in*

me, and I in him. As the living Father sent me, and I live because of the Father, so whoever feeds on me, he also will live because of me. This is the bread that came down from heaven, not like the bread the fathers ate, and died. Whoever feeds on this bread will live forever." Jesus said these things in the synagogue, as he taught at Capernaum (John 6:47–59).

This story loses its power when we get distracted by discussion of what it does not mean. Because of the historical debates of the High Middle Ages and Reformation surrounding the rite of the Lord's Supper, we miss the point of the whole thing.

Jesus is the bread of life. He gives his life to us for food. He lived his life in such a way that it became life for us. He provided his life to be life for us. He is the bread of life, broken on the cross, now being distributed throughout the world.

Because Jesus bled and died on the cross and was raised from the dead in the power of the Holy Spirit, we can partake in the resurrection life of Christ. By faith and in a mystery, the flesh and blood of Christ, broken and spilled at the cross and resurrected by the power of the Spirit on the third day, are the source of our new resurrection life.

The laws of the kingdom call us to live like the King, and King Jesus never eats his people. He feeds them. Even giving himself, his very life, to feed them. All kingdom living is summed up in this: Be like Jesus. There is no abstract list of rules. There is Jesus, who has given himself to be food for us. His life is ours because we are in him.

We are kind to one another, we feed and care for one another, and we refuse to bite, devour, and consume one another because Jesus is the King, and he has lived that way. Because you have a kind King, living as a citizen of the kingdom of God means living in kindness.

Kind Like God

Be kind to one another, tenderhearted, forgiving one another, as God in Christ forgave you (Ephesians 4:32).

Kindness is a rare commodity. We use the word. We can't define it.

It was a hot day on a dusty back street in Tijuana Mexico when I told a group of boys outside of a little market that I wanted to put a bottle of Coca Cola in my cow. *Yo hablo un pocito Español.* And *vaca* and *boca* got mixed up in my limited vocabulary. I understood that I had said something funny. They were all laughing and repeating it to one another. The cow noises while they drank their Cokes let me in on the mistake.

Language proficiency degradation is no secret. Perhaps that is why the label of kindness is tossed and taped the way it is? Our culture is like the linguistic non-native me in Mexico, trying to put soda into the livestock. As one of your own poets has said, "You keep using that word. I do not think it means what you think it means."

We assume that we know a virtue like kindness. We use the word all of the time. But many of us are not native speakers when it comes to virtue. Many of our kindnesses are anything but.

What, then, defines kindness? I contend that kindness is acting well on a desire to see a flourishing life in our friends, family, or enemies.

For the Christian, though, none of life's virtues are abstractions. The Apostle Paul tells us that we should be kind to one another because God is kind (Ephesians 4:32). Kindness is defined by the person of God. All of the works of God are done by a kind God. Any Christian pursuit of kindness must begin with the question of who God is and what he has done.

First and foremost, God has revealed himself to us through his son Jesus. God is kind. Jesus is the full revelation of God to us, and therefore, if we want to know kindness, we must look at God the Father, and his only begotten son, Jesus Christ. Defining kindness can be difficult. At least if decisive practicality is our goal. But we are not called to follow abstract definitions and the rules of the virtue of kindness. We follow Jesus. We imitate him. And, since he is kind, we learn what kindness is by looking at Jesus, who is kind.

At the end of Ephesians 4, Paul puts God's mercy at the center of his kindness. Mercy is not treating a person according to their sins. Mercy requires being able to see a sinner, see what they deserve, then to actively not give them what they deserve. Forgiveness is an act of mercy. "*Be kind to one another, tenderhearted, forgiving one another, as God in Christ forgave you"* (Ephesians 4:32).

As you look at Jesus, the Scriptures make it plain that mercy is absolutely essential and central to kindness. Jesus' kindness is filled with mercy.

But God's mercy towards us is a beginning. His mercy towards us is the engine that drives our kindness towards one another. Since almost everyone you will ever deal with in this life is going to be a sinner, continued kindness requires mercy.

Mercy does not treat a person according to his sins. Mercy see a sinner, see what they deserve, then actively does not give them what they deserve. But to do that, we need and have a rationale other than the reasonings of vengeance. Vengeance gives people what they deserve because they deserve it. It lives in a 'give-what-you-get' posture. Everything we do weighs the scales of what we deserve for us or against us.

I worked in a high school for kids coming out of juvenile detention. One of my high school students was trying to explain to me why he was so convinced that, despite some of the evidence, he was actually a good person.

He said, "Just this morning, while I was driving to school, I stopped as a lady was crossing the road in front of me. I could have run her over right there, but I didn't. The way I see it, I could kill someone after school today and still be even."

Balancing the scales will always end in cruelty. But mercy sets aside vengeance. It sets aside scale-balancing. To take on a posture of mercy we will need to drop scale-balancing.

If we are going to become, and then remain, merciful people then there are two things that we need to keep before our mind. First, God is better at vengeance than we are. Second, we have received far more mercy than we generally realize.

First, God is better at vengeance than we are. We can be merciful because God takes care of vengeance that needs to be taken care of.

> *Repay no one evil for evil, but give thought to do what is honorable in the sight of all. If possible, so far as it depends on you, live peaceably with all. Beloved, never avenge yourselves, but leave it to the wrath of God, for it is written, "Vengeance is mine, I will repay, says the*

Lord" (Romans 12:17–19).

Vengeance is not our job.

We can drop our attempts at scale-balancing and live peacefully with everyone (as far as it depends on us) because God takes care of vengeance. Our mercy is by faith. Every time we return kindness for evil, mercy for sin, or love for enmity, we are acting in faith that God will set all things right in the end. His justice is pure and complete. Ours is not.

Every malevolent response reveals our lack of faith. We are acting as if God will not keep his word and be all the avenger that we need. Believing that Jesus, from his great white judgement throne, will set all things right in the end looks like mercy towards friends, enemies, and strangers.

Mercy, rather than vengeance, is trusting God to be our deliverer. Solomon tells his son, *"Do not say, "I will repay evil"; wait for the Lord, and he will deliver you"* (Proverbs 20:22). So not only will God's judgment put all things right in the end, the Lord is at work putting things right within history as well. He is the God of vengeance who shows himself as such in history (Psalm 94:1).

How often do we look at someone sinning against us and act as if they are getting away with something? There is no getting away with anything. If someone is sinning against us we should want to overcome their evil with good so that their sin is overcome. If someone is sinning against us, it is not as if their sin is bad for us and good for them. Sin is slavery. Sin is self-destructive. We ought to love our enemies (whether permanent or temporary enemies) and desire their rescue from sin, even if that sin is against us.

Kindness can only be merciful by continually remembering that God is the judge who will take care of vengeance. But that is only half way to motivation. Motivation to not sin is not the same thing as motivation to do what is right. So where does motivation to be merciful come from? It comes from seeing that we have been the recipients of more mercy than we could ever give.

We become merciful when we learn to live before God as someone in need of mercy and see that God's generosity is anything but tightfisted.

One of the spiritual blindnesses of the Pharisees was the inability to see themselves. They lived lives without mirrors. Their perceptions of themselves were warped in their favor, and so they believed they were the moral superiors of the sinners that lived up and down their street.

There was a Pharisees that invited Jesus to dinner. But his expected dinner guest surprised him by attracting a notorious sinner. She showed up at the Pharisee's house looking for Jesus. She came into the dining room while they were at the table. She knelt at his feet and wept uncontrollably. It seems to have made everyone except Jesus terribly uncomfortable. Her tears fell so hard and flowed freely enough to wash Jesus' feet with them. After she wiped his feet clean with her hair she kissed his clean feet and poured an expensive bottle of perfumed oil on them.

But she was a sinner. The Pharisee invited Jesus for a calm theological discussion. He knew that no self-respecting prophet would put up with such a notorious reprobate. And this one was kissing and massaging his feet.

Now when the Pharisee who had invited Him saw this, he spoke to himself, saying, "This Man, if He were a prophet, would know who and what manner of woman this is who is touching Him, for she is a sinner."

And Jesus answered and said to him, "Simon, I have something to say to you." So he said, "Teacher, say it."

"There was a certain creditor who had two debtors. One owed five hundred denarii, and the other fifty. And when they had nothing with which to repay, he freely forgave them both. Tell Me, therefore, which of them will love him more?" Simon answered and said, "I suppose the one whom he forgave more." And He said to him, "You have rightly judged."

Then He turned to the woman and said to Simon, "Do you see this woman? I entered your house; you gave Me no water for My feet, but she has washed My feet with her tears and wiped them with the hair of her head. You gave Me no kiss, but this woman has not ceased to kiss My feet since the time I came in. You did not anoint My head with oil, but this woman has anointed My feet with fragrant oil. Therefore I say to you, her sins, which are many, are forgiven, for she loved much. But to whom little is forgiven, the same loves little (Luke 7:39–47).

Our mercy-meter is calibrated by our take on God's mercy to us. If we believe that we generally have it together, that we have not been as needy as some of God's other children, then kindness will flow from us like molasses on a cold day. If we believe that God's mercy has been reluctant, that God is scroogey with his love, then we will be stingy to give love and mercy. Our kindness directly correlates to how kind we believe God is with us.

In fact, how merciful we are with people is a better indication of what we truly believe about God than what we tell people our official theology is. We show that we believe God is merciful by being merciful. We show our faith that God is kind be being kind. As James says, "Show me your faith apart from your works, and I will show you my faith by my works" (James 2:18b). The way that we treat people is what we actually believe about God. As Job tells his counselors, *"He who withholds kindness from a friend forsakes the fear of the Almighty"* (Job 6:14). A failure of kindness is bad theology.

God is always merciful and kind. It is not something that comes and goes. It is the way that he is. *"The Lord is righteous in all his ways and kind in all his works"* (Psalm 145:17). His kindness does not waver. He does not wait until we are good enough, or wait until we have proven ourselves and then begin to be kind. He is kind from beginning to end and from top to bottom.

God is not a bureaucrat at the front of a DMV line waiting for us to get the right form stamped and the right information together before we can have our allotted amount of earned kindness. He is not kind because of who we are or what we have done. He is kind because of who he is, and he never slumbers nor sleeps.

Remember when we were in Egypt and worshiped the gods that we found there? When, after we had seen the arm of the Lord stretched out to save us, after the ten fingers of God's hands destroy every one of the gods of Egypt, one plague at a time, we saw the Red Sea pile itself up on either side of us to make way for our escape. And then we watched the Red Sea pile itself onto our enemies as they tried to follow us through it. We still turned to a golden calf made by our hands rather than trust in God.

And what was our God's response to our hardheartedness?

> *But they and our fathers acted presumptuously and stiffened their neck and did not obey your commandments. They refused to obey and were not mindful of the wonders that you performed among them, but they stiffened their neck and appointed a leader to return to their slavery in Egypt. But you are a God ready to forgive, gracious and merciful, slow to anger and abounding in steadfast love, and did not forsake them* (Nehemiah 9:16–17).

God is kind and merciful to us even at our worst. And so we should follow him by being merciful ourselves.

Kindness is neither calculating nor vengeful, but is merciful. Kindness does not return fire.

But it is not enough to refuse to return fire. Kindness is both merciful and on top of that, it is forgiving.

> *Be kind to one another, tenderhearted, forgiving one another, as God in Christ forgave you (Ephesians 4:32).*

We are kind to one to another by forgiving one another

We are not called to pursue kindness in the middle of an outpost of elite angelic community. Paul assumes that we are going to be rubbing shoulders with sinners. And to these offensive jerks he says, be kind. And in fact, he lumps you and I right in with them. He says forgive *one another*, which assumes that you are and I are all going to need forgiveness.

If you find yourself frustrated or surprised at yourself when you sin then you may need to face down your own pride. Have you ever sinned and then thought, 'What the heck? I'm better than that.' A slap from a friend is better than a kiss from an enemy. Let me be your friend. You are not actually better than that.

It is a trap to sin and then beat yourself up after

for failing to meet your inflated vision of yourself. Do not be surprised by your own sin. Expect it. Prepare for it. If you are humble and expect to need to be forgiven then you will be ready to admit your faults and ask for forgiveness.

There is not a better way to prepare to forgive than to prepare to be forgiven—because kindness requires forgiveness. Kindness is not something that can only exist in a sinless environment. Kindness *is* forgiving. And a forgiving kindness can change the atmosphere of even the most sin-marred relationship.

But what exactly is forgiveness?

Sin exists between persons. Sin is a relational reality. Sin gets between people and disrupts fellowship. ***Forgiveness is the setting aside of sin by the offended party and the promise to not treat the person according to their sin.*** It is objective and involves the restoration of the relationship. We are to forgive *ONE ANOTHER*.

This is how it works. In a fit of rage you call your neighbor an imbecile who could not mow in a straight line to save the Titanic from disaster. You extend to him one fifth of a wave. Your sin has injured your relationship. It is between you and your neighbor and between you and God, in whose image your neighbor is made. It is objectively there as a broken relationship.

But God calls us to acknowledge our sin. So you say "God, will you forgive me for my disrespect for your law, my failure to be kind, my mean-spirited outburst of wrath and my selfish abuse of my neighbor."

God forgives you because Jesus died as the propitiation for your sins on the cross and was raised from the dead by the power of the Spirit. God forgives us and our relationship with God is restored.

Then you go to your neighbor and acknowledge your sin ask for forgiveness "Mr. neighbor, will you forgive me for my mean-spirited outburst of wrath and my dishonoring of your lawn-mowing abilities, I acted out of envy and I was trying to hurt you. Please forgive me.

He says, "I forgive you." Now the relationship is objectively restored. The forgiveness is objective. It is not just a feeling. It is a gift and a promise. "I forgive you," is a promise to act as if it never happened. It is a promise to objectively forget the sin and a promise not to bring it up with anyone else.

We are able to do that when we are tenderhearted towards one another. *Be kind to one another,* **tenderhearted,** *forgiving one another.*

When Paul encourages us to be tenderhearted, he is telling us to be ready to forgive. That is what tenderhearted means.

God is ready to extend forgiveness. *"For You, Lord, are good, and ready to forgive, And abundant in mercy to all those who call upon You."* (Psalm 86:5, NKJV). Paul is simply calling us to be good disciples of Jesus, living our lives limiting his.

Tenderheartedness is the opposite of hardheartedness. Compassion, sympathy, and pity are not sins. We should not avoiding them like we do. Survival-of-the-fittest self-centeredness has no place in the church.

Hardheartedness is an ugly sin. God looked at us and had pity on us. He then calls us to look at each other, not with hard hearts that see weakness as a place to gain supremacy over each other, but instead sees others with a tender heart that is full of compassion.

A tenderhearted person is looking for ways to forgive. They will say, "I forgive you" faster than a toad gets off a hot griddle. A tender heart sees the weakness of a person laying themselves down in the vulnerability of repentance and responds with compassion, not imagining themselves superior. A tenderhearted person loves to set aside offecnces, forget sins, and restore relationships (Isaiah 43:25).

I have taught at a handful of different schools and have seen countless little ones have to ask for forgiveness. I remember one little brunette with glasses. She was in the first grade and she had been disrespectful to one of the teachers from another classroom. She was dragging her feet reluctantly as she held her teachers hand and walked down the hall from her class to the door of the next class down. The teacher came to the hall and, as she defended herself by only showing the top of her head, she said, "Will you please forgive me for being disrespectful during the assembly?"

The teacher got down on her level and said, "I forgive you. I love you." And gave her a hug. She received the hug with shoulders slumped. But after the hug, she looked at her teacher with a little crooked smile, straightened her glasses, and turned to skip back to her class.

What would have happened had the teacher refused to forgive her? Or said, "I forgive you. But you are always disrespectful. I don't want to see you being disrespectful anymore."

I can tell you what would have happened, because I have seen it. She would have stayed slumped and blobbed back to her class. Most likely, she would have been in trouble again later in the day.

A relieved conscience is tender. A guilty conscience will grow a rhinoceros hide, and eventually the horn too.

Often we act as if we will lose respect if we are quick to forgive. Reality is the exact opposite. The quicker and more completely a person forgives the more respected they will be. *"If you, O Lord, should mark iniquities, O Lord, who could stand? But with you there is forgiveness, that you may be feared"* (Psalm 130:3–4). God's way to respect is tenderhearted forgiveness. God forgives us over and over and it is his forgiveness that changes us.

Jesus regularly seems to overextend mercy. Convicted in a monkey trial on trumped up charges, convicted by lying witnesses, beaten, mocked, spit on, nailed to a cross and left to die he prayed, "Lord Forgive them, they know not what they do."

A woman that was caught in the very act of adultery was dragged into the middle of town and thrown in front of Jesus. After talking her accusers off the edge, he turns to her and says, "I don't condemn you. Go and sin no more."

He is merciful beyond what seems reasonable.

I grew up in Spokane, Washington. You knew it was winter because frozen water floated from the sky and gathered in white piles all over everything. In Santa Cruz the sun shone. Christmas decorations were winter's only monogram. To convince ourselves Old Man Winter was awake, we would car-hunt for the best Christmas decor. At one house that was particularly well decorated—blow up Rudolph on the roof, full size baby Jesus with the whole family, lights that you could probably see from the edge of the atmosphere—my six-year-old daughter professed,

"Wow! I love it when people overdo Christmas."

Jesus seems to overdo mercy. And forgiveness. And grace. And kindness. And this is Paul's motivation to be kind by forgiving.

"Be kind to one another, tenderhearted, forgiving one another, as God in Christ forgave you" (Ephesians 4:32). When we forgive, we are saying that we will no longer treat someone according to that sin. We put aside the sin and any vengeance that we believe is owed us. Why? Because God, when our death was owed, when vengeance for our faithlessness was deserved, sent his son Jesus to die in our place so that he could forgive us.

Paul has us calculate forgiveness with a new formula. We do not only look at the other person's sin. We look at whether or not God has forgiven us. He has. Then we treat the people that have sinned against us the way that God has treated us.

So here's the deal, if you have a hard time forgiving, it is because you are self-righteous. You do not understand how much God has forgiven you. Our grace for other people is a reflection of our understanding of the grace that God has shown us.

Only when we focus in on the sins that have been committed against us, forgetting the context of the overwhelming grace that surrounds us on every side, are we able to hold onto offenses and not forgive. When we act like sins committed against us are such a big deal, we are creating our own miniature world where we are the gravitational center. Any grace we show will pale in comparison to the grace that was shown to us when Jesus came and died on the cross for us. Forgetting that drains our ability to give grace.

It grieves the Holy Spirit when we mistreat and use people. When we are harsh and selfish with people, when we are unforgiving and hardhearted, we are ignoring the direction of God's Spirit. The only way that we can continue in our harsh, selfish, and unforgiving way of living is by forgetting the good news of Jesus' death and resurrection. That is the true context of all of our life.

Words that Build

Let no corrupting talk come out of your mouths, but only such as is good for building up, as fits the occasion, that it may give grace to those who hear. And do not grieve the Holy Spirit of God, by whom you were sealed for the day of redemption. Let all bitterness and wrath and anger and clamor and slander be put away from you, along with all malice. Be kind to one another, tenderhearted, forgiving one another, as God in Christ forgave you. Therefore be imitators of God, as beloved children. And walk in love, as Christ loved us and gave himself up for us, a fragrant offering and sacrifice to God (Ephesians 4:29–5:2).

Take one step back now from the Ephesian command to be kind like God and let's look at the context. Paul points to another mountain that kindness should conquer: our tongue.

In Paul's day one of the major struggles in the church, in families, and throughout the community was the way that people talked to one another.

Not much has changed in 2000 years.

In high school, my father's business partner hired a friend and me to rid his property of an old shed. We showed up with sledge hammers, pry bars, and two long hexagonal wrecking bars piled in the back of my little gray Mazda pickup truck.

We started on the roof, splintering and breaking off wood with our pry bars. Then we took the sledge to the walls (taking turns, since it was the fun part) and then tore each fallen wall into scrap with the wrecking bars. We piled the scrap lengthwise on the side of the garage until there was no shed, only wood.

We came without hammers and nails. Our belts

had no tape measures. We had no need for a screw gun. They were unnecessary. We had no plans to build anything.

For many of us, the people in our lives are sheds to tear down, and so our words are simply tools of destruction. We are not planning to build anyone up, and so we stuff our tool-belt with unkind words and jump in. In the Ephesian church in Paul's day, this was a serious problem. The speech of the people of God was tearing down rather than building up. But Paul tells them to *"Let no corrupting talk come out of your mouths, but only such as is good for building up, as fits the occasion, that it may give grace to those who hear"* (Ephesians 4:29).

Words are powerful. God made us able to talk because he wants us to use words to give grace. God wants us to use words the way that he did in creation. God used words to build a world and a garden in order to give it to Adam and Eve and all of their descendants. He used his words to give love and favor. His words were gift-building words.

The Ephesians, on the other hand, were using the

power of their words to tear down and destroy one another. This grieved the Holy Spirit who had sealed the church for the day of redemption (Ephesians 4:30). Paul wanted them to put all harsh bitterness, wrath, anger, argumentative clamor, and slander away, along with all malice (Ephesians 4:31).

As you speak, your words are building a habitat for the people around you. If the way that you speak makes people want to move away, then your words are building haunted houses.

Build comfortable and comforting places. Learn to build safe places with the way that you speak.

Even if you can never afford that big beautiful house on the hill, you have everything that you need in the way that you speak to build a house that people want to be in. Better is a single bedroom shack with kind speech than a mansion filled with harsh words.

Paul tells husbands to be specifically careful to not be harsh with their wives (Colossians 3:19). A husband should be building up his wife. He should build strong walls around her by honoring her with his words. Many husbands expect their home to transform into a tunnel of love even though they have been building a woodshed with their words all day.

Many wives fail to understand that Paul admonishes them to respect their husbands because their husbands need to be built up by their words. A wife that is harsh and judgmental, who tears down her husband when she speaks to him, is often frustrated by how weak her husband becomes. She might even double down on her attempts to make sure her husband understands his failures, not realizing that what he needs is to be built up by her words.

Because we are made in the image of a God who creates with words, we are created able to build up or tear down with words. Paul tells us that every time the Ephesians spoke to one another in bitterness, spoke harsh and destructive words, were wrathful and angry, or impatient and slanderous, they were speaking against the Spirit that had sealed them.

Their words were clamorous and slanderous and full of malice. Their words were destructive, tearing down those that God was building up by the power of his Spirit.

They were not just tearing down any old building. The people that they were speaking to were temples of the Holy Spirit (1 Corinthians 12:13; Romans 8:9). They were taking their crowbars and sledgehammers to the Holy Spirit's temple. Dangerous business.

Instead, God's Spirit calls them to be kind to one another. *"Be kind to one another, tenderhearted, forgiving one another"* (Ephesians 4:32a). They were to use their words to build one another up. Paul knew that God was calling them to be kind to 'one-anothers' who were sinners. Thus, kindness is going necessarily to involve forgiving one another.

If, then, they are going to be prepared to use their words to build one another up, they cannot be hardhearted. They are going to need to be tenderhearted, prepared to forgive, glad to forgive, and quick to forgive with their words. There will not be any other way to continue working on our word-built neighbor.

God began by speaking our neighbors into existence. We are to continue building them into the stature and fullness of the image of Christ Jesus by building them up with our tenderhearted words of kindness and forgiveness.

Of course, we will never answer God's invitation to be a part of this neighbor-construction if we are only responding to the way that we are treated. When we look at how we are handled and respond accordingly then we will sustain and extend the sin-revenge cycle. Instead, we are told to treat one another in response to the way that God has treated us in Christ Jesus. *"Be kind to one another, tenderhearted, forgiving one another, <u>as God in Christ forgave you</u>" (Ephesians 3:32).*

God has forgiven you, so forgive one another. You have been shown grace, so you show grace. God has been kind to you, so show kindness to one another. This is what the second commandment is about.

> *You shall not make for yourself a carved image, or any likeness of anything that is in heaven above, or that is in the earth beneath, or that is in the water under the earth. You shall not bow down to them or serve them, for I the Lord your God am a jealous God, visiting the iniquity of the fathers on the children to the third and the fourth generation of*

those who hate me, but showing steadfast love to thousands of those who love me and keep my commandments (Exodus 20:4–6).

We are never to serve God at any image that we make. We do not return our thanks or our service to an image we made because we are to return our thanks and service to the Image of God that God has made. Our neighbors are made in God's image and so we return our thankful service to God towards them.

My wife was in the hospital to deliver our fourth child during the Christmas season. Sitting chatting with our delivery doctor, our doc said, "I love delivering babies. Every baby reminds me that God's son became a little baby just like this."

Each person is made in the image of God just as Jesus is the image of God. In fact, Jesus could become a descendant of Adam without losing his identity because we are made in the image of God, and he is the eternal image of God.

Anyone you meet is an Adam or an Eve. As descendants of Adam and Eve they are images of God. There is no part of the image lost in the begetting.

When God commands us to not make any graven images, it is not because he does not want us to serve him at images. It is because he has provided us with living images of himself already. We do not serve God at graven images. We serve him by serving our neighbor, who is his image.

As Paul goes on, he explains that, because God has forgiven us in Christ, we should "*Therefore be imitators of God, as beloved children" (Ephesians 5:1)* As a well-loved child imitates his parent, we are to imitate God. If we want to know what God is like, then we look at Jesus, because Jesus is the full revelation of God to us. If we have seen Jesus, then we have seen the Father. God has been revealed to us in Christ. To imitate God, then, is to be as Christ is to us towards one another.

Thus, we are to love one another.

> *Walk in love, as Christ loved us and gave himself up for us, a fragrant offering and sacrifice to God* (Ephesians 5:2).

We love one another how Jesus loved us. Jesus gave himself away for us, and we love one another that same way. We give ourselves away for one another. That is what Christ did for us. We are to look at the way that Christ has treated us and treat one another accordingly.

This is by far one of the most difficult commands in Scripture, but notice that the motivation is that Christ was a sacrifice, and his sacrifice was a fragrant offering to God.

He gave himself up for us on the cross. Mind, body, and soul all given for us. The Father desires our salvation and Jesus' glorification. He calls us to follow him into and in this self-giving love.

C.S. Lewis, in *The Four Loves*, explains that it is an unfortunate turn of phrase to say that a man trolling the bars is looking for a woman. He is, Lewis points out, "not looking for a woman at all. He is looking for a pleasure for which a woman happens to be a necessary apparatus. And sadly one doesn't 'keep the carton after one has smoked the cigarettes' so to speak." Love, if it is love, does not seek its own; it seeks the good of the one it loves.

Love, according to a scriptural definition, however, is not a passive emotional response. Love is aggressively giving yourself away for the good of another. It is aggressive in that it actively seeks for the good of the loved. It is a giving of one's self and the primary gift that is given in love is "me."

We are called to be imitators of Jesus by giving ourselves away for one another, and we can do that because Jesus already gave himself for us. His giving of himself pleased the Father. Jesus gave himself as a sacrifice and we are called to follow him into sacrifice. We are called to imitate him, giving ourselves for one another.

We are never called to make sacrifices. We are called to be sacrifices.

When we use our words to destroy people, we are not giving of ourselves, we are taking from others. Sometimes we think that, by taking from others, we are building ourselves up. But what our word-chomps take from others will not become a part of us. What we take with harsh or violent words is simply sluffed off at the end of the day. They are emptied and we are not any more full.

Our words can tear down where God is building. When we let bitterness and resentment grow up in our relationships, when we let outbursts of anger and wrath, noisy clamor and useless arguments, go unconfessed in our homes, or at work, or in our church, we are not building up; we are tearing down.

There is a water beetle that eats frogs alive. To be more precise, in drinks frogs. But unlike the spider that injects a fly with poison to get it to stay still while it is devoured, it just wraps the frog up and overpowers it. It then snaps its sharp snout through the skin of the frog and uses its straw like proboscis to gulp and swill the inner frog until there is nothing left but empty frog.

When we use words to tear down, we are taking the self of another. Rather than giving ourselves for them, we are taking and using them for ourselves. When our words are harsh and cruel and violently destructive we are forgetting the violence that was committed against Christ on the cross on our behalf.

When we shame, intimidate, guilt trip, or speak with malice and evil towards one another, we are forgetting that Jesus was nailed to a cross and hung naked for us. We are forgetting that his complete offering of himself on the cross for our sins was a sweet smelling sacrifice.

When we tear one another down with our words, we are forgetting that that the Holy Spirit sealed us until the day of redemption.

But God can transform the way we speak. He can and does restore his image in his people so that they quit using the power of their words to tear down and become people that build with their words. But he does not do it by laying new laws and rules upon us until the pressure of the guilt finally forces us to obey. Instead, he transforms our desires, making us want to be people that speak with kindness.

We have all been failures at using our words to build. It is tempting to think that now we simply muscle our way into speaking with more kindness. But notice what is embedded within this command. This command is a Gospel Command. This command rests on the reality that God is kind and has forgiven us.

If God is not overflowing with love for you, then this command becomes meaningless. In fact, if this command feels like a heavy burden, then you are misunderstanding it. This is the kind of command that should lighten your load. It is an easy yoke that you can only take up if you drop the heavy yoke that you have been wearing.

Have you been using your tongue to tear down? Have you been harsh and unkind? Have you blown it? Have you yelled at your kids? Have you yelled at your parents? Whatever your sins, bring them to Christ. Lay them down.

If your life seems too heavy to carry it might not be your life that is too heavy. It might be your death. It might be the weight of the shame and guilt of your unconfessed sins. Lay your sin at the cross.

Jesus died so that you could find all your sin and shame and guilt has been taken away. In Christ we are clean. In Christ we are forgiven. Trust the good news embedded in this command. *Be kind to one another, tenderhearted, forgiving one another,* **as God in Christ forgave you.**

Lay your sin on the cross and be forgiven. Forgiveness is for sinners. Healing is for the sick. The Good News of Christ's death and resurrection; the good news that our sins have all been taken away, the Good News that Christ's death can make the foulest clean, is all good news for sinners. If you are a sinner, then you qualify.

If you hold onto the shame of your past then you will not be able to be kind. Lay it aside. When you let your sin pile up, it is like dropping bricks into a backpack. You stick them in one at a time and they never seem that heavy individually. Your load does not seem to get that much heavier with each brick. But it is not long before you are walking with a slouch and your legs are aching with the extra pressure.

Do not let the guilt of what you have done imprison you. That was why Jesus was put on trial and found guilty when he was innocent.

Stop allowing the things that you have done make you feel dirty and ashamed. That was why Jesus was made to carry his cross covered with dirt and sweat and blood.

Do not be chained by the thought that because of who you are and because of your sin you would be better off dead. That is why Jesus died on the cross.

Because Jesus' sacrifice was accepted on our behalf, your guilt, and shame, and fear are all taken away. Jesus' blood atones for our sin. We can know that we are accepted. Jesus was raised from the dead. There is no greater sign that we are free to live the life that God is calling us to. We can be kind to one another, and tenderhearted, because God, in Christ, has forgiven us.

Get Rid of All Bitterness

See to it that no one fails to obtain the grace of God; that no "root of bitterness" springs up and causes trouble, and by it many become defiled (Hebrews 12:15).

There are certain kinds of spiders that do not have stomachs. When it is time for them to eat, they inject their digestive juices into their still living victim, secreting digestive enzymes that break down the body of their prey. They then suck up the liquefied flesh-pulp before secreting another load of stomach acid, repeating the back and forth, in and out, with the digesting flesh until the victim is an emptied shell or the spider is done eating.

How often do we let bitterness take root and become like these spiders. We let our bitterness so color the way we see someone that in our harsh selfishness we bite and devour them. We digest them while they sit in front of us, and all the while, because of our bitterness, we tell them that they deserve it.

Guilt is what we feel when we sin. Bitterness is what we feel when others sin against us. Bitterness is resentment come of age and ready to settle down in in the suburbs with a white picket fence. Bitterness grows when someone sins against you (or you think that someone sins against you) and you resent what they did. Then you hold onto that resentment until it changes how you look at that person.

You do not want to be bitter, but sometimes it is difficult to realize that you are bitter. So how do you know if you are bitter? There are a few signs.

Maybe you make a face like you just put horseradish root in your mouth or you spit on the ground every time someone's name is mentioned.

Or maybe you display inappropriate amounts of emotion for the size of an issue, no matter the issue, with a particular person.

Can you recall all of the details of something that happened six years ago? The key to memory is repetition. Bitterness remembers all the details because it repeats the details over and over as it lets the resentment get buried deeper and deeper.

Bitterness is often manifest as complaining, spitefulness, explosions, slandering, or reveling in someone's disasters.

Sometimes we can get a better understanding of what something is by investigating its antonym. What is the opposite of bitterness?

Tenderheartedness: Tenderheartedness is ready to forgive. Tenderhearted people do not use their neighbor's treatment of them as motivation; they use God's treatment of them as motivation.

That is what the parable of the wicked lender is all about. The man that owed the king a hundred million dollars was forgiven his debt but started beating his servant who owed him five dollars.

He could have retreated to the facts. "He really does owe me five dollars." But he is not supposed to be looking at his servant to decide how he is supposed to act. He is supposed to be looking at how God has treated him and then act according to God's grace. God never acts bitter with us. He is always tenderhearted and forgiving. Even when we sin against him, he is patient and forgiving and tenderhearted.

Remember how Paul put it:

> *Let all bitterness and wrath and anger and clamor and slander be put away from you, along with all malice. Be kind to one another, tenderhearted, forgiving one another, as God in Christ forgave you* (Ephesians 4:31–32).

As we have seen, we are to look at the way God has treated us in Jesus, which is tenderhearted, and in kindness, and with forgiveness, which is the opposite of acting bitterly. We are to treat each other the way that God has treated us. If we are to do that, we *have* to get rid of all bitterness.

We need to, "*See to it that no one fails to obtain the grace of God; that no 'root of bitterness' springs up and causes trouble, and by it many become defiled*" (Hebrews 12:15).

Bitterness acts like a root, a root that produces fruit, and the fruit of bitterness is defiling. When you are bitter, you are a threat to everyone around you because bitterness accumulates. It accumulates within a person, it accumulates groups of people around it, and every evil work follows on its heels.

Bitterness destroys community, it destroys relationships, and it destroys the people that you are close to. When we hold on to bitterness, that root grows poison fruit. We become a source of defilement. When we let the root of bitterness grow up, we feed people the poisonous apples that grow from that root. We are like Snow White's witch as we pass out the fruit that grows up in a bitter heart. Hebrews tells us, bitterness leads to every evil work. When we spread our bitterness, we are spreading evil works.

If you stay bitter, then you cannot share it. It defiles the people around you. But you cannot just hide it away inside either. Because even if you never see the root of a tree directly, you can know that it is there because it is lifting and cracking up the sidewalk.

There are maple trees that were planted all along the sides of the roads on the sides of the South Hill of Spokane where I grew up. When the trees were first planted, there were not yet asphalt paved roads or cement sidewalks. The roads were red brick and there were grass and dirt paths along the side of the brick streets. You still find some of the horse troughs being used as flower beds that have been there since the roads were first put in for the horses that would pull the carriages under the beautiful maple canvases.

The bricks have since been replaced by asphalt and the sidewalks have been paved. One of the unforeseen consequences of the maple-lined streets is the incredible root systems that grow and develop under each giant maple tree.

Years of maples growing between the road and the sidewalk has produced slabs of concrete that are lifted, turned, and broken beyond usefulness. Along the sides of some hills they looks more like stairs than sidewalks.

Roots can be covered up, but they cannot be hidden long term. Roots eventually make themselves known either with fruit or by breaking up the surface from underneath.

You are not able to share your bitterness without defiling those around you. You are not able to hide your bitterness away without cracking up from the inside. Yet, you are not allowed to simply embrace it, enjoy it, or brag about your bitterness.

> *But if you have bitter jealousy and selfish ambition in your hearts, do not boast and be false to the truth. This is not the wisdom that comes down from above, but is earthly, unspiritual, demonic. For where jealousy and selfish ambition exist, there will be disorder and every vile practice* (James 3:14–16).

Devils glory in their bitterness. Demons stew in their resentment. They throw all the "perceived" sins against them in the crock-pot and start the slow boil. But we must not imitate the demons. Bitterness causes confusion and leads to every vile and evil work. Evil follows bitterness because bitterness becomes our excuse for doing terrible things to people. We use bitterness to justify our sin.

"She deserves it . . ."

"I know that I did it, but he . . ."

Bitterness clouds our judgment and becomes our justification for the evil things that we do. Think of Simon the Magician in the book of acts. He repents and is baptized, but then he sees the power that God has granted to the Apostles. He tries to purchase the power of the Holy Spirit from the Peter. Why would purchasing God's power seem like a good idea? Because, "he was in the gall of bitterness" (Acts 8:18-23). Every evil work follows on the heel of bitterness.

The root of bitterness depends on the soil of selfishness. It needs our self-centeredness to grow. It cannot survive in the soil of self-giving kindness.

If you make your decisions by asking "What do I need?"; if everything you do is to get what you think you need; if the only time you do something for someone is to try and get them to do what you want (even if they never know that that is why you are doing it), then you are setting yourself up for bitterness.

If you always act what *you* want, then you are probably already bitter. If you are not yet, then you are on your way there. Every time that you catch yourself trying to manipulate your spouse or your children or your parents, or anyone; when you catch yourself trying to manipulate someone by being nice, or doing something for them, stop and say "God please forgive me for being selfish and teach me to be a servant in my heart as well as my hands."

The best way to get rid of bitterness is to go after the soil that the root grows in. If there is no selfishness for bitterness to take root in, then your bitterness will die of starvation.

When a starfish is going to eat a clam it wraps itself around the clam and begins prying open the shells. Even though a clam has one of the strongest muscles in the sea, once the starfish is attached, it relentlessly pulls and pries until it sneaks open the hard shell guardian. And then the starfish shoots its stomach into the clams where the clam's tongue and soft tissues are all snug and supple.

The starfish then wraps up the tender innards of the clam with its stomach and begins digesting. It grasps and absorbs the clam's interior by digesting and swallowing it until it is dead.

How often are we the starfish, limbs of suckers wrapped and pulling in order to crack open and fill our family and friends and neighbors and coworkers with our digestive guile--and all in the name of what they have done to us.

Bitterness is a canker. Bitterness has tentacles that sprawl into everything. Bitterness has fangs full of poison, and when allowed to mature, it bites indiscriminately. That is why Paul insists that we get rid of all bitterness.

If you are not allowed to enjoy your bitterness, and you cannot act on it, because what will come out is evil, and you cannot share it, because you will defile everyone around you, and you are not able to keep it inside because you and the world around you will start to crack up like an old sidewalk, then what can we do with our bitterness?

We have to get rid of it. We have to bring it to

God the Father through Jesus. We have to have it yanked out, down to the deepest roots. We have to repent of it. We will talk about what that looks like in the next chapter, but we will never become kind or loving people if we harbor bitterness and resentment.

Bitterness' grip is like a giant Venus flytrap. We are here, but we are being digested alive. There is only one thing that will help us and that is God granting us the grace to bring the sin into the light.

Bitterness is the kind of sin that can hide under the carpet for years and all that anyone notices is a faint smell of something rotting. No one can put their finger on it, but you can tell that there is something dead somewhere. We need God to grant us the strength to haul it out into the open.

If you are bitter, then you need to confess your sin to God and you need to ask him to forgive you. If you are bitter and have been acting on it, then you need to confess your sin to everyone that you have defiled. Our hope is not in the darkness, but in the light. Despair follows the hiding of sin; joy follows the confession of sin.

Parenting with Kindness

And as you wish that others would do to you, do so to them. If you love those who love you, what benefit is that to you? For even sinners love those who love them. And if you do good to those who do good to you, what benefit is that to you? For even sinners do the same. And if you lend to those from whom you expect to receive, what credit is that to you? Even sinners lend to sinners, to get back the same amount. But love your enemies, and do good, and lend, expecting nothing in return, and your reward will be great, and you will be sons of the Most High, for he is kind to the ungrateful and the evil. Be merciful, even as your Father is merciful. "Judge not, and you will not be judged; condemn not, and you will not be condemned; forgive, and you will be forgiven; give, and it will be given to you. Good measure, pressed down, shaken together, running over, will be put into your lap. For with the measure you use it will be measured back to you (Luke 6:31–38).

Parenting is an impossible task. You are unprepared, under-skilled, and unqualified for the venture. You are simply unable to do what needs to be done.

When God calls us to walk an impossible road there are a number of possible responses. We work harder, thinking that we will be able to power through our limitations with gumption, techniques, and the right methods. We go to parenting conferences and read books, getting whiplash as we bounce from ditch to ditch trying to stay on the road.

Or, it is impossible—out of my control— and therefore must be one of the deep mysteries of the universe. When he created me with limitations, God tied my hands, so parenting is a cosmic crapshoot. We cry uncle and trust to luck—ahem, I mean, the inscrutabilities of providence.

But there is a third option. We can live from faith to faith, embracing our limitations as another opportunity to live by faith. We continue our Christian life the same way that we began it. There are only two ways to raise kids: by faith or by works.

When we are called to an impossible task, like parenting, we must embrace it by faith. In such a task, our works will always fall short. And so we parent by trusting God and following him. We can take up our cross and follow God to the table and hearth.

Parenting, like all of the Christian life, is about imitation. We imitate God. We imitate those that are imitating God. And in imitation we discover both our own individuality and our place in God's economy.

But the imitation does not stop there. Our children will then imitate us. This sounds terrifying but it is a design feature. It would be frightening and depressing, if it were not for the fact that God is also our Father. So we have him with us first as a loving father, acting on behalf of us and our children. Second, we have him with us as an example, since our parenting should be an imitation of his fatherhood.

In fact, the reason that there are even fathers at all is because we are made in the image of a God who is *the* Father. *"For this reason I bow my knees to the Father of our Lord Jesus Christ, from whom the whole family in heaven and earth is named"* (Ephesians 3:14–15).

The first place that our children learn what God like is from their parents. We set our children's expectations for God's nature.

But there is another father in the world, the father of lies.

> *You are of your father the devil, and the desires of your father you want to do. He was a murderer from the beginning, and does not stand in the truth, because there is no truth in him. When he speaks a lie, he speaks from his own resources, for he is a liar and the father of it* (John 8:44).

Parenthood is not a universal cleansing agent. It is not enough to be a parent. The devil is a parent too. He is the father of lies.

The form of parent must be filled with the

content of the imitation of God the Father. Your children will learn from you what God is actually like, or they will learn lies. We need to know God's character.

In Luke 6, Jesus explains what it means to follow him. The morality of Christianity is radically different than other ethical systems in the world, and not just in content. There are significant differences in content—and two of the most radical requirements that Jesus makes of his followers are here in this passage—but there is something even more radical.

The word radical comes from the Latin *radix*, which means root. The ethical root is different for Christians. Jesus, just like the entire Old Testament, teachers that true morality is a matter of imitating God.

The ethics of the Bible are about following a person. It is not a list of rules. The law is a description of God. It is not about an abstract list of right and wrong that can be deduced rationally or discovered through observation of natural law.

God does not change, and so morality is a constant throughout the ages. There is no moral relativity in the ethics in Scripture. We know right from wrong by looking at God and what he has revealed to us of himself. His character and attributes can be listed, but you can never separate morality from who God is. He is true and good and beautiful. He is the standard. When we want to know right from wrong, we look at God.

Jesus begins his sermon in Luke about the fatherhood of God with the Golden rule. "*And as you wish that others would do to you, do so to them*" (Luke 6:31).

This is an important principle for parents. Would you want to be treated the way that you are treating your children?

Your children are people. Do not talk about them in ways that you would never talk about another adult. Do not speak to them in ways that you would not talk to another adult. Treat your children the way you would want to be treated.

The justification is going to be, "Because this is what God is like" (v. 35). As you treat your children like people, think of the way that God the Father speaks about Jesus. When Jesus is being baptized, or when Jesus is on the mount of transfiguration and the Father opens up the heavens over Jesus, he says, *"This is my beloved Son, in whom I am well pleased"* (Matthew 3:17).

We want him to say over us what he said over his only-begotten Son. The pleasure of God over us is our motivation to want to continue to be faithful to God. This is how God our Father is with his children. We should imitate this in our own parenting.

Your children need to work from your pleasure in them, not to your pleasure in them. As a parent, do unto your children what you want your father in heaven to do unto you. To embrace us as children and to be pleased with us, not because we have done all that he asks and have become perfect children, but because we are his children. We can trust that our father is with us, bringing us along, teaching us the ways of the family that we are securely adopted into.

Embrace your children the way that you want to be embraced and loved. We begin by saying, "these are my children. I love them. I am pleased by them. I am proud of them."

Your children should be motivated by the fact that you are pleased to have them as your children.

In Matthew 25, that is how Jesus motivates us. I know that you want to hear the Father say, "Well done, my good and faithful servant." Be faithful. Do not give up. The Father is watching and when you stand before you he will say, "Well done."

Our "well done" should mean something to our children. If they are confident and secure in our love, it will. Our love should not shift based on whether or not they are doing everything that you ask of them. Our love should not waver based on how well our children are obeying us.

This is how Jesus puts it.

> *If you love those who love you, what benefit is that to you? For even sinners love those who love them. And if you do good to those who do good to you, what benefit is that to you? For even sinners do the same. And if you lend to those from whom you expect to receive, what credit is that to you? Even sinners lend to sinners, to get back the same amount* (Luke 6:32–34).

If you love your kids when they love you, what credit is it to you? Remember, Jesus says that love looks like obedience: *"If you love me, you will keep my commandments"* (John 14:15). If you only love you your kids when they obey you, what credit is that to you? The worst sinner is able to love their children **back**.

When your children are acting cute and being good they are easy to love. When your children are not loving and obey you, that is when parenting like God the Father will stand out. That is when the difference between God the Father and the father of lies becomes apparent.

> *But love your enemies, and do good, and lend, expecting nothing in return, and your reward will be great, and you will be sons of the Most High, for he is kind to the ungrateful and the evil. Be merciful, even as your Father is merciful* (Luke 6:35–36).

When your kids are being thankless, when your kids will not obey, when your children are being rebellious, at that point you need to respond with kindness.

When you fly off the handle, when you get frustrated and grind your teeth at your children, you are grinding their souls with a lie about God the Father. Remember that God is kind to the thankless and evil.

When my four kids were all under seven, we were driving in our minivan to a meeting. My kids were snacking on yogurt so that they would be able to, hopefully, survive without meltdown. They started giggling and I smiled at how wonderful my children were. When the giggling turned into full-fledged belly laughter I wanted to know what had them laughing so hard. At which point there was a thud and the laughter all stopped.

The laughter stopped just long enough for them to each take a breath deep enough to howl with laughter like a group of baboons warning the jungle canopy that a black panther was on the prowl. I risked it and looked back. The yogurt was all on the ceiling of the van.

I yelled.

There was yogurt on the roof of the van. (Yogurt which left a stain that was still there when we sold the van years later.) I did not respond with kindness. Not even a little bit.

I smiled benevolently when my children were being cute. As soon as their joyful exuberance destroyed my property I was a jerk. They splattered yogurt. I splattered their little souls all over the ceiling of the van.

I had to ask for forgiveness because, of course, I needed my kids to forgive me for sinning against them. But also because that meeting that we were heading to was a meeting about parenting. I was teaching. One of the things I was teaching on was, *"Brothers, if anyone is caught in any transgression, you who are spiritual should restore him in a spirit of gentleness. Keep watch on yourself, lest you too be tempted"* (Galatians 6:1).

We are called to a gentle kindness in our parenting. Kindness that expects nothing in return. Kindness looks at the way that God the Father is kind and merciful. Kindness that and treats our children with that same kind gentleness.

Of course, our kindness does not ignore sin in our children. Kindness sees sin and deals with it, but kindness aims at bringing relief to the pressures of guilt and shame through forgiveness and acceptance. It does not use guilt or shame as a tool to gain mere outward obedience. Kindness never settles with behavior management.

God is firm and kind to the thankless and evil. He does not give whatever we want, whether it is good for us or not. God is neither manipulated by our thanklessness, nor does he respond with manipulation. Instead, his kindness leads us to repentance (Romans 2:4).

When you respond by laying a guilt trip to get your children to do what you want rather than dealing with the heart of the matter, or when you respond by rewarding their thanklessness or evil, you are missing key opportunities to show kindness. God deals with us in kindness by calling us to ask for forgiveness. By loving us by working into us a motivation of loving wisdom and loving obedience.

God works into us thankfulness and respect by forgiving our sin. "*But with you [God] there is forgiveness, that you may be feared*" (Psalm 130:4).

He does not press us to do the things that he

wants us to do and then restore us once we have proved ourselves. He forgives and changes our hearts with his kindness. We become people that honor him because he has already restored us with his forgiveness.

When, in kindness, you aim at relieving your child's sin—teaching them to ask for forgiveness, and forgiving them—then you are motivating like God. Then you are cleaning the inside of the cup in order to get the outside clean.

Guilt trips are remarkably shortsighted. As soon as the guilt-giving influence is gone the motivation will dry up. Guilt motivation dissipates faster than a wet spot on the beach in the middle of a hot summer day.

Only if the motivation to do what is right wells up from within will continue to flow when you are not around. An actual desire to do right, rather than a desire to avoid guilt or manipulating preassure, is the only thing that lasts.

If our kindness is like God's, then when our children are thankless, disobedient, and doing what is wrong, our kindness will not be passive. It will lead them to repentance.

"Honey, your attitude is thankless. Ask for forgiveness, so that we can put it behind us."

Kindness is tenderhearted, loving to forgive. And that means that, as parents we are leading our kids, teaching our kids how to deal with sin, and how to ask for forgiveness, so that we get to forgive them.

But you cannot give what you do not have. If we are going to be a blessing to our children, helping them deal with their sin through confession and repentance then we need to be dealing with our own sin in the same way.

> *Judge not, and you will not be judged; condemn not, and you will not be condemned; forgive, and you will be forgiven; give, and it will be given to you. Good measure, pressed down, shaken together, running over, will be put into your lap. For with the measure you use it will be measured back to you* (Luke 6:37–38).

When you are parenting, you need to have a much harder and higher standard for yourself than for your kids. As you are being renewed in your mind, take the opportunities to let your children know that you are struggling against sin along with them.

One of the best ways that you can teach your children how much you love forgiveness, and how much they should love forgiveness, is by asking for forgiveness from them when you sin against them, and then thanking them for forgiving you. When they see that you are glad to confess your sin and be forgiven, they will learn that it is easier to confess and seek forgiveness than to try and hide their sin.

They should not think that you think you have it together, that they are the little strange animals because they still sin. Be humble. As you guide them to repentance, do not be a condemning judge getting his kicks out of catching and criticizing.

Instead, love forgiveness. Love to reach out and embrace, and forgive and forget your children's sin.

Remember how God deals with your sin.

> *I will arise and go to my father, and I will say to him, "Father, I have sinned against heaven and before you. I am no longer worthy to be called your son. Treat me as one of your hired servants.'" And he arose and came to his*

father. But while he was still a long way off, his father saw him and felt compassion, and ran and embraced him and kissed him. And the son said to him, 'Father, I have sinned against heaven and before you. I am no longer worthy to be called your son.' But the father said to his servants, 'Bring quickly the best robe, and put it on him, and put a ring on his hand, and shoes on his feet. And bring the fattened calf and kill it, and let us eat and celebrate. For this my son was dead, and is alive again; he was lost, and is found.' And they began to celebrate (Luke 15:12–24).

Every time someone turns from sin, confesses, and returns, this needs to be your response. This is how true fathers—fathers that reflect the fatherhood of God—are with their children.

The measure that God uses to bless is not a teaspoon, but a snow shovel. We never out-bless, out-mercy, or out-give God. His measure is too large.

The quicker you are to forgive, the quicker guilt is put aside, the quicker someone will repent and ask for forgiveness next time around. Repentance should be encouraged, and God encourages repentance with kindness and forgiveness. God's kindness leads us to repentance because he is tenderhearted and ready to forgive. He wants to get to the business of enjoying one another's company in fellowship.

Receivers Give

And you were dead in the trespasses and sins in which you once walked, following the course of this world, following the prince of the power of the air, the spirit that is now at work in the sons of disobedience-- among whom we all once lived in the passions of our flesh, carrying out the desires of the body and the mind, and were by nature children of wrath, like the rest of mankind. But God, being rich in mercy, because of the great love with which he loved us, even when we were dead in our trespasses, made us alive together with Christ--by grace you have been saved-- and raised us up with him and seated us with him in the heavenly places in Christ Jesus, so that in the coming ages he might show the immeasurable riches of his grace in kindness toward us in Christ Jesus. For by grace you have been saved through faith. And this is not your own doing; it is the gift of God, not a result of works, so that no one may boast. For we are his workmanship, created in Christ Jesus for good works, which God prepared beforehand, that we should walk in them (Ephesians 2:1–10).

Kindness is the point of redemption. Kindness is the point of what God has done. When we were under the curse of death, by nature begotten in wrath, God wanted to be kind to us.

Though cursedly incapable of receiving his kindness, God sent his son Jesus to bring us new life. New life in Christ adapted us to receive his kindness.

The first kindness was resurrection life, which make us able to handle every other kindness that God pours on us.

When we come to this passage in the second chapter of his letter to the Ephesians, Paul is helping us to remember the greatness of God's grace. But he begins by reminding us of the condition that we were in when God got hold of us. We *were dead in the trespasses and sins* (v. 1). We trespassed. We crossed a forbidden line. In the Garden of Eden we trespassed when we ate the fruit that we were told to avoid (Gen. 3:6). We were trapped under the curse of death. The wages of our sin is death, and so we are born under the curse of death. We are born living in death.

But we were not only born under the curse of death. We make a return on Adam's sin by walking according to the sinful desires of our heart. We followed after the dead life of our desires and passions. We wanted sin. Our bodies wanted sin. The world simply provided an arena for our sinful desires to find fulfillment. We were born as sons and daughters of wrath, just like every other descendant of Adam and Eve (v. 2-3).

We were not just in need of a boost up. We were dead. We were in need of resurrection. We were dead because, born in sin, we have deliberately chosen to continue in sin and death rather than following God.

Paul reminds you to remember your story. Remember? You are a descendants of Adam and Eve. You sinned on purpose and loved it. Remember? You embraced your desire for sin and made innovative returns on it, even developing new creative ways of sinning. Remember?

You and I, we are all sinners born of sinners. We have all spent our time and energy in sin. You came from there too.

> *Among whom we all once lived in the passions of our flesh, carrying out the desires of the body and the mind, and were by nature children of wrath, like the rest of mankind* (Ephesians 2:3).

Christians are not people that were generally better than the rest, seeing that following Jesus was another good thing to do. We were stuck, dead, unable to save ourselves.

> *But God, being rich in mercy, because of the great love with which he loved us, even when we were dead in our trespasses, made us alive together with Christ--by grace you have been saved* (Ephesians 2:4-5).

What we could not do, God did. He did it because he is rich in mercy. He did it because he loves us. Even when we were dead in sins, when we were not doing anything to make it look like a good idea to save us, God came to us and brought us new life when he raised Jesus from the dead.

By grace, and only because of God's grace, we are saved from sin and death.

Our salvation is all gift. None of it is because of anything that we did, or do. If God had stopped right there it would have been enough for us. But the gift giving does not stop.

God is rich in mercy, and he is generous. Not only does he give us new life, he gives us a seat with Christ. The reasoning here is still surprising every time I read this passage. He wants us in a place where he can continually pour the riches of his kindness on us.

> *And raised us up with him and seated us with him in the heavenly places in Christ Jesus, so that in the coming ages he might show the immeasurable riches of his grace in kindness toward us in Christ Jesus* (Ephesians 2:6-7).

He draws us near so that he can show us his kindness throughout the ages. When God draws you to himself, it is not because he wants to smack you around for a bit. He wants you near so that he can show you the depth, breadth, and width of his kindness.

Is your definition of grace large enough? Or is your word grace a wineskin that needs to be burst by reality?

It is not because you have begun to figure it out, or because you know the secret password, or because you have at least done a few of the things that you should be doing. It is because God has come with a gift.

Even the ability to receive the gift is a gift from God.

> *For by grace you have been saved through faith. And this is not your own doing; it is the gift of God, not a result of works, so that no one may boast* (Ephesians 2:8-9).

Faith is trusting God's promises because of who God is. Faith is the way that we grasp onto the gracious gift that God is giving us. Faith is the way that we take the promises of God as our own. At the end of the day, even the ability to believe is something that we turn around and say 'thank you' for.

Salvation should humble us. There is nothing about our salvation that should cause us to look at other people and sneer. Our salvation is pure charity. It is overflowing generosity from our kind and merciful God.

Everything about our salvation is a gift. Jesus said that our ability to show love and compassion to those around us is a good meter for how well we have understood God's grace. Our ability to love those that God puts in front of us is directly related to our understanding of how much God has forgiven us.

As this grace flows into us, stopping to pool as gratefulness, it will flow out of us in good works.

> *For we are his workmanship, created in Christ Jesus for good works, which God prepared beforehand, that we should walk in them* (Ephesians 2:10).

God is gracious to us, and, as the pure gift of God's grace comes to us, we can actually go out and be gracious and kind. As you come to understand how gracious God is to you, how much sin he has forgiven, how much sin in you he has covered with the blood of Jesus, then you will become a loving person.

If you are constantly piling the guilt onto the people around you, if your family sees you coming and flinches because you are going to lay into one of them, if you are unkind, and unloving, if people are crushed under the weight of your constant criticism, then ask yourself, "Am I treating the people around me the way God has treated me?"

God is gracious and kind; TO YOU. He did not treat you according to your sins. He did not hold your sin over you in condemnation and bitterness. If he brought up all of your sins, you would never be able to stand. If you are always bringing up peoples sins and failures, they are never going to be able to stand. No one could.

So stop being the train of condemnation that

crushes everything in its path. Look at God's grace and forgiveness and know that you were created for these same kinds of good works.

If you have been a jug that pours condemnation all over everyone, when you realize it, your temptation will be to turn on yourself and drink the whole jug down yourself.

Don't.

Turn to God and confess it, "Father in heaven, I've been unloving, unforgiving, impatient, condemning. Please forgive me."

When you confess your sins, God is faithful and just to forgive your sins. God forgives you. Jesus died on the cross because you are a screwed up sinner that needs grace constantly. He does not condemn you.

Be filled up with his mercy so that you can pour the mercy that has been poured into you.

Legal Hatred

And Pharisees came up and in order to test him asked, "Is it lawful for a man to divorce his wife?" He answered them, "What did Moses command you?" They said, "Moses allowed a man to write a certificate of divorce and to send her away." And Jesus said to them, "Because of your hardness of heart he wrote you this commandment. But from the beginning of creation, 'God made them male and female.' 'Therefore a man shall leave his father and mother and hold fast to his wife, and the two shall become one flesh.' So they are no longer two but one flesh. What therefore God has joined together, let not man separate." And in the house the disciples asked him again about this matter. And he said to them, "Whoever divorces his wife and marries another commits adultery against her, and if she divorces her husband and marries another, she commits adultery." And they were bringing children to him that he might touch them, and the disciples rebuked them. But when Jesus saw it, he was indignant and said to them, "Let the children come to me; do not hinder them, for to such belongs the kingdom of God. Truly, I say to you, whoever does not receive the kingdom of God like a child shall not enter it." And he took them in his arms and blessed them, laying his hands on them (Mark 10:2–16).

Divorce is a painful topic. This passage from Mark's Gospel receives some of the most emotionally charged interpretations of any passage in the Bible. That makes sense. Questions about marriage strike to the heart of our identity. They cut to the quick about our most fundamental motivations.

There are two kinds of motivations in the world. Two ways to look at the God's word. Two ways to look at our lives. Like pharisees or like disciples. A pharisee looks at himself and asks, 'What is the least painful way that I can get what I want.' It is self-centered. God may come into it, but God becomes one more tool in my self-fulfilled project. It is self-love, turned in on itself, and out for itself.

Jesus presents another way of living, another way of seeing, another way of being. Instead of self-interest and self-love, he calls us to be motivated by our love of God. Instead of looking first at our desires, living to fulfill our own agenda, Jesus says, "Come and follow me." Instead of using God and our neighbor for our agenda Jesus invites us into his agenda. He calls us to lay our self down and take up Jesus' mission for the world.

There was a machinist that worked for the Ford Motor company early in the company's history who had been stealing tools. After he was baptized, he returned them. He explained that he had recently become a Christian and asked for forgiveness for stealing from the company.

The manager that received both the tools and the confession was unsure what to do. This was a first. He sent a cable to Mr. Ford, who was visiting a

European factory, explaining the situation and asked what to do.

His response was, "*Dam all of the Detroit River, and baptize the entire city*."

If baptism and conversion to Jesus would make his employees honest then he would be glad to use it to his own advantage. He was glad to have Jesus as a supporting actor in the story of his company.

The Pharisees approached Jesus to see if he could take a supporting role in their agenda. Jesus was on his way to Jerusalem. Many Jews and even some gentiles were convinced that Jesus was the long promised Messiah. But the important people were still trying to get a handle on Jesus' agenda. Still undecided on Jesus, Pharisees came to him with a question about divorce. So they come with a question to determine which political camp he lands in.

The Pharisees were the conservative nationalists, hoping to restore Israel. In their version of the story, Israel had fallen from glory. She used to be free and self-governed. Israel had always been taxed, but before they had been conquered by Gentiles, at least all of their taxes had stayed local. Now their taxes went to the Empire. Once their government had been limited by law. Now their freedom was limited by force.

The Pharisees believed that Israel's exile was retribution from God for disobedience. They believed that Israel's restoration depended upon obedience to God's law.

When they interrogate Jesus, we learn that they had the wrong end of the stick. They brought their own agenda to God and said, "OK. What do we need to do to get our nation back?" In their obsession with their own agenda they missed out on God's agenda. God's plan came walking into their front yard. Instead of dropping everything to follow him, they squinted their eyes, tilted their heads, and gave the Messiah a theological exam.

They checked if Jesus would be a benefit to their agenda by asking for his thoughts on divorce.

> *The Pharisees came and asked Him, "Is it lawful for a man to divorce his wife?" testing Him. And He answered and said to them, "What did Moses command you?" They said, "Moses permitted a man to write a certificate of*

divorce, and to dismiss her (Mark 10:2-4).

So far so good. Except Jesus knows that they are missing the law's purpose. The law limits sin. The civic laws (laws dealing with relations between neighbors) deal with minimum requirements and limiting the civic effect of sin. It does not describe the ideal life.

When Moses makes this allowance for divorce, permitting it in certain circumstances, he is not therefore saying that divorce can be a good thing as long as the laws are kept in the process. The fact that there is a law allowing divorce does not mean that divorce is therefore commendable.

Keeping the divorce laws is not the endgame of marriage.

Jesus hears their question, but he uses it to point out that they are confused about the way God's Word should be used. They have showed up to play baseball, and they have all of the right equipment, but they are pitching the bat and trying to hit it with the ball. They have confused what the law is about and have misunderstood what it means to live.

Jesus corrects their misunderstanding of the purpose of the Bible. The book of Genesis is our archetype. The Garden of Eden, before sin entered the picture, is our example of what marriage is supposed to be.

> *And Jesus answered and said to them, "Because of the hardness of your heart he wrote you this precept. But from the beginning of the creation, God 'made them male and female.' For this reason a man shall leave his father and mother and be joined to his wife, and the two shall become one flesh'; so then they are no longer two, but one flesh. Therefore what God has joined together, let not man separate* (Mark 10:5-9).

Divorce is not what God intended for marriage. Laws about how to dissolve a marriage are for sinners.

Of course, in spite of how straight forward this is, the disciples are confused. After they withdraw from the public eye, they ask for further explanation. Jesus explains that you can obey the letter of the law and still be in sin.

In the house His disciples also asked Him again about the same matter. So He said to them, "Whoever divorces his wife and marries another commits adultery against her. And if a woman divorces her husband and marries another, she commits adultery (Mark 10:10-12).

You can file all of your divorce papers properly, you can get a perfectly legal divorce, but getting a divorce in order to marry someone else does not keep you from adultery.

Many people will approach Jesus' declaration about adultery here in the exact same spirit as the Pharisee's original question. If we think Jesus is merely disagreeing with the Pharisees about the rules of litigation, we have learned exactly nothing. Instead of growing as a disciple we end up being the best Pharisee for Jesus that we can be.

But Jesus is actually saying that marriage is not about providing the legal minimums for your spouse. Marriage is a relationship of love and loyalty. It is about giving yourself to someone that is not like you. As a husband and wife give themselves in love to one another, honoring and loving one another, they are reflecting the self-giving love of God. Kindness never retreats into litigious correctness, because legal hatred is still hatred.

The love of God is never given in bare legal minimums. He loves with an ungrudging delight. He gives gifts and joys far beyond the bare minimums. Just think of how delicious the world is. Or how beautiful it can be. Are sunsets and fresh salsa bare minimums? Is hot coffee on a foggy morning necessary?

Love never stops at mere gifts. God goes so far as to even give himself. This is what both Christmas and Pentecost are about.

When Jesus became a man, when he was born of the virgin Mary, God was giving himself. Jesus is the eternal Son of God, the complete and perfect revelation of the Father. God the Father dwells in him and he dwells in the Father.

To receive Jesus is to receive God the Father. This is, in fact, the great and glorious good news. We can receive God and God can receive us because Jesus became a man.

Often we even think of the gospel in terms of how

it can fulfill the agenda that we have for our own lives. If I want good kids, I ask if the gospel will get me good kids. If I want money, I inquire if the gospel will get me the money that I am after. If I feel bad about myself I inspect the gospel to see if it will counteract my existential angst.

But the Gospel is our restoration with God achieved *by God*. God has revealed himself in Jesus. The good news is that we can know and be known by God.

> *"Let not your hearts be troubled. Believe in God; believe also in me. In my Father's house are many rooms. If it were not so, would I have told you that I go to prepare a place for you? And if I go and prepare a place for you, I will come again and will take you to myself, that where I am you may be also. And you know the way to where I am going." Thomas said to him, "Lord, we do not know where you are going. How can we know the way?" Jesus said to him, "I am the way, and the truth, and the life. No one comes to the Father except through me. If you had known me, you would have known my Father also. From now on you do know him and have seen him." Philip said to him, "Lord, show us the Father, and it is enough for us."*

> *Jesus said to him, "Have I been with you so long, and you still do not know me, Philip? Whoever has seen me has seen the Father. How can you say, 'Show us the Father'? Do you not believe that I am in the Father and the Father is in me? The words that I say to you I do not speak on my own authority, but the Father who dwells in me does his works. Believe me that I am in the Father and the Father is in me, or else believe on account of the works themselves* (John 14:1–11).

In the incarnation of Jesus, God gave us himself, but he also has given himself in the gift of the presence and ministry of the Holy Spirit. God has made his people into the temple is which he lives. "*. . . you are God's temple . . . God's Spirit dwells in you?*" (1 Corinthians 3:16). And each Christian is a temple of the Holy Spirit. "*. . . your body is a temple of the Holy Spirit within you, whom you have from God . . .*" (1 Corinthians 6:19).

God has gone far beyond any minimum legal requirements and given us himself.

When we think of our love and kindness for one another in terms of accomplishing legal minimums, what is allowed and not allowed, rather than in terms of faithfulness and loyalty, we ignore the shape of God's kindness towards us.

God never deals with us by meeting the bare minimums. He has gone out of his way to think up ways to bless us.

Not because we first loved him, though. He came to us when we do not love him. His love for us is not taken up with this insipid and little souled attitude that the Pharisees bring to Jesus. God's love is generous and overflowing, not because we are worthy and lovely, but because he is going to make us lovely. His lavish openhandedness towards us makes the Pharisees look like little miserly scrooges in their singular stinginess. They are frisking Moses to make sure that their hatred is legal in the eyes of God. God has sent his own son to die in order to open up the pathways of his kindness.

So the disciples should not be like the Pharisees, but what should they be like? The answer is waiting at the door.

> *Then they brought little children to Him, that He might touch them; but the disciples rebuked those who brought*

them. But when Jesus saw it, He was greatly displeased and said to them, "Let the little children come to Me, and do not forbid them; for of such is the kingdom of God (Mark 10:13-14).

Often these two stories are treated separately, but these children burst into the house in the middle of the conversation. They are the perfect example. Instead of being like the litigious and stingy-souled Pharisees, the disciples need to become like these little children.

> *"Assuredly, I say to you, whoever does not receive the kingdom of God as a little child will by no means enter it." And He took them up in His arms, laid His hands on them, and blessed them* (Mark 10:15-16)

The Pharisees and the Disciples had been coming to Jesus, testing him, asking his opinion about divorce, trying to figure out what the minimum they needed to do in order for divorce to be legal and proper. Jesus says, "Quit acting and thinking like divorce lawyers. Come to me like children. Come ready to be loved, blessed, played with, and enjoyed."

The Kingdom of heaven, the rule of earth by Jesus, is not a bureaucracy. The kingdom is not a heavenly city hall where we spend all of our energy standing in lines and getting our forms stamped and signed properly. It is a family. We are the children and God is our father. We gather to God because he loves us and we want to be blessed and embraced by his love.

This is a completely different way of looking at the kingdom of God. *"See what great love the Father has lavished on us, that we should be called children of God! And that is what we are!" (1 John 3:1a).*

The Pharisees were missing the whole point. They were thinking that once they got the rules all straight then God would look at them and say, "Good work. You have passed the Kingdom of Heaven's BAR exam. Now you can be kingdom lawyers."

Jesus pick up the children and says, "This is what it looks like to be a disciple rather than a pharisee." To not be priggish and rulish and concerned with earning God's favor. To not think in terms of bare minimums and what you can get out of a situation, always scheming to make sure that your hatred is legal.

Instead, a disciple think in terms of how much they can give. How much they can love. They look at what they have and think, "This is how much I have to lay out" like Children playing tag.

When you watch children play tag they will run with all of their hearts. That is what makes for a great game of tag. Not because if you get tagged everything falls apart and the world ends. The fun is running with your hardest. You do not need a rule that everyone gets to punch you in the head if you get tagged to get kids to run harder. You run with all of your heart for the joy of a great game of tag.

Jesus says, "Follow me. Come be a part of the kingdom of God. Here you can give everything in your pursuit of God."

And the Pharisees say, "What is the minimum?"

They are the kid that wants to stand over in the corner of the field thinking that if no one notices them that they are winning at tag. Or worse they are the kid that is always trying to massage the rules in his favor rather than just playing the game with his whole heart. They want to give the minimum and still get what they want.

But a disciple says, "Everything? I can lay out everything? That sounds wonderful. Help me Lord to give it all."

Stop thinking of love and kindness in terms of bare minimums. Instead, look for ways to do be like God. He has gone far above and beyond the bare minimums, even giving us his very self, so that we could be adopted into his family. He has removed every obstacle between us and his everlasting kindness.

When I Don't Want to be Kind

The difference between an orange and an orangutan is not a four-letter syllable. Though the words look and sound similar, the realities that they represent have nary a thing in common. When I hear someone say that they are not actually interested in people being kind to them, I wonder if we are at oranges and orangutans.

"Perhaps we are talking about different things?"

"Nope. I am not interested in pity. I don't need my life sugarcoated. I just want the plain truth. I don't need kindness. I'll take life straight."

"Ahhh. Orangutans and Oranges."

"Huh?"

Two people using the same sounds is not a guarantee that they are talking about the same thing.

Sometimes people reject kindness because the only kindness that they have known is the unkindness of false friends. People who have been surrounded by the kindness of rivals, always wagering for the upper hand and manipulating for the advantage, are not kind. But neither the buttering of a salesman nor the promises of spineless politeness are true kindness.

David tells us that he has no interest in the politenesses of the wicked because he loves kindness.

> *Do not let my heart incline to any evil, to busy myself with wicked deeds in company with men who work iniquity, and let me not eat of their delicacies! Let a righteous man strike me--it is a kindness; let him rebuke*

me--it is oil for my head; let my head not refuse it (Psalm 141:4–5a).

He would rather be punched in the face by his friends than to hear the simpering and delicate words of the wicked. A face full of fist from a friend that knows you need it is kindness.

There is nothing as excellent as a friend who is kind enough to rebuke you. David knows that it is hard to hear kindness when it comes in a backhand. He prays that God will help him receive it when it comes, but true kindness knows when to drink tea and when to ring the Round One bell.

So sometimes people say that they are not interested in kindness because they think oranges when kindness is an orangutan.

In fact, kindness is the proper soil for rebuke to grow from. When a kind person rebukes a friend as a friend, it is often not even taken as a rebuke. The words are taken in the spirit of the kindness that has always been the atmosphere of the friendship. Kindness sees a friend in sin and recognizes the potential of that same person without the chains.

Kindness is willing to say the hard things that need to be said because they have hope that the possibilities will become realities if there is just the freedom to stretch.

How often have you rebuked out of sheer meanness hoping to sting rather than bless. Hoping, not to help someone, but to help someone feel stupid. A kind rebuke has faith in God for someone when they are not able to have it themselves. Kindness sees for its blind friend. The rebuke of a friend is a kindness. Those that reject kindness for straight talk are actually rejecting hopeful straight talk that builds for hopeless straight talk than shatters.

Other times, people reject kindness because they know that they are unworthy of receiving kindness themselves. It would be wasted on them and so they reject kindness as a category.

There was a coffee shop a few miles from where I grew up that had terrible customer service. You could go in and be sneered at, ignored, and generally treated as a nuisance.

Once I asked for a toasted bagel and the employee said, "You can have a bagel, but not toasted." I asked why, thinking that something must be wrong with their toaster.

He said, "It takes a long time. I don't want to deal with it right now."

There was no one in the cafe, no one else even in line. He looked at me, acting like refusing to toast my bagel was a completely normal and rational thing for someone in his situation. Yet there was generally a long line of regulars gathered to buy coffee from a rude barista. The guilty feel a bit better when someone slings a bit of incivility their way. Especially first thing in the morning.

When we believe ourselves too guilt-ridden—too contemptible—for simple kindness, then a pinch of churlish impudence with your morning coffee fits. That which fits puts you at ease.

But the problem is, when you begin living in search of what you deserve, you start giving people what they deserve. You enter a cycle of vengeance and revenge. If you should receive unkindness for your sin then you will believe that everyone else should receive unkindness for their sin. This pernicious merry-go-round has no exit.

"Kindness makes me uncomfortable. I don't deserve it. Instead I will gather to myself the uncaring."

Sadistic humor, savage cynicism, and spiteful sarcasm become the norm when we simply return what is owed.

Christians will even spiritualize our heartlessness with an appeal to depravity. "We are all sinners getting better than we deserve. A little realism is probably good for people."

There is nothing more real than God, and God makes the sun shine and the rain fall on the just and the unjust alike. His kindness is simply unrelated to what we do or do not deserve.

God hitches our neighbor-kindness to his kindness. We owe our neighbor kindness because God has been kind to us. No matter who God puts in front of us, we owe them kindness simply because they are made in the image of the God who has been kind to us.

> *"Owe no one anything, except to love each other, for the one who loves another has fulfilled the law"* (Romans 13:8).

It is illegal, breaking the law of God, to be unkind to our neighbors. Whether family, friend, or even our enemy (Matthew 5:43-48), because they are made in the image and likeness of our kind creator. We owe our creator loyalty. Loyalty looks like loving our neighbor.

We reject the kindness of others when we lose track of God's character. Kindness dies on a balance sheet.

What about when we do not actually want to be kind? When we want to lash out and hurt people. Or when we want to ignore people. When we want to freeze people out, like a wart on your middle toe.

We always do that which we most want to do. Because of sin, our desires conflict with one another. Sometimes it is a small thing. I want both to have money in my pocket and I want a lime snow cone. I am not able to have both, and so we have to choose between an empty pocket and a lime snow cone in my hand or a pocket full of quarters and empty hands.

Other times the desires at odds are significant. There are times that we want to be kind, and yet we also want something at odds with that kindness. Like revenge. If Dostoevsky has taught the world anything, it is that spite is a powerful and ever-present motivation. Each of us has within us the seeds of our own destruction—a sinful desire to reap death, to shatter and subjugate our neighbor, to glory in the downfall of our friends and enemies alike. We are sinners who do not always want to be kind.

What do we do with the meanness of our own souls? What do we do when we find anger, wrath and malice in our own hearts? Paul's tells us to kill it. *"Put to death therefore what is earthly in you. . . But now you must put them all away: anger, wrath, malice. . ."* (Colossians 3:5a, 8a).

We have to kill it. Put it off. Mortify it. We have to set out to get rid of it. God never settles for simple behavioral management. By the power of the Holy Spirit, God changes our desires. A change of behavior alone is paltry. In the death of the old man, our love is steadily realigned with what God loves.

In fact, behavioral change without a change in your desire injures your soul. It divides your psyche. In concentrating on behavioral management and performance containment, without desire renovation, we dislocate our very selves.

Paul teaches us that one of the marks of godliness is an undivided simplicity (2 Corinthians 1:12). Behavior detached from desire ruptures souls. But God's action and desire are never ruptured. When God acts, all of God is present in the act. God has the undivided simplicity that Paul is urging us towards. As Augustine writes, "In the Eternal… nothing passes away, but the whole is simultaneously present" (Confessions, 11.11.13). To serve the Lord by serving our neighbor we must serve with an undivided simplicity in which our whole self is present in every act. We should have a simple and undivided heart that wants to do what we are doing (Ephesians 6:5-7), not merely worrying about modifying our behavior, for the sake of appearances.

This is part of our restoration. The Father, in

Christ, and through the Spirit, is reconstructing us into the image of himself, our Trinitarian Creator, Redeemer, and Sustainer. The reordering of our desires is included. *"Set your affection on things above. . ."* (Colossians 3:2a). That is why Paul never tells us, "just ignore your desires and do what is right." We are being rehumanized, rebuilt, renovated back into what God intended for us. The remodel includes our desires. All of who we are is being returned to the image of God.

Jesus, the one through whom God created the world, became a complete man. A complete—and completely innocent—man, including his desires, died on the cross, and was raised from the dead. When we are united to him, all that we are, including our sinful desires, was nailed to the cross. Everything that he is, including his perfectly ordered desires, becomes ours by faith.

In baptism we are covenantally joined to Christ Jesus (Colossians 2:12). His death becomes our death. His Life becomes our life. His resurrection becomes our future. By faith we press into Jesus' life, into Jesus' image, so that it becomes our life now as well.

Our desires are being fundamentally transformed by this new identity. By faith, his righteousness, his death, and his resurrection have become ours by our union with him. So also his desires should become ours desires as well. This is what it means to live by faith.

When you don't want to be kind. Look back at the cross and remember the nails that pierced your desire to do evil. Look forward to the day when your desires will be perfectly aligned with truth, beauty, and goodness and you want both what Jesus wants and how Jesus wants. Let that truth be the context, and, by faith, pursue life by pursuing kindness.

Kindness by Faith

Do not lie to one another. Seeing that you have put off the old self with its practices and have put on the new self, which is being renewed in knowledge after the image of its creator" (Colossians 3:9b–10).

Faith banks on God's promises. Living by faith means trusting that God will do what he promises. But a promise is, by definition, something that has not yet happened. Faith, then, lives the future into the present.

We will be raised from the dead when Christ returns at the end. That resurrection life—that we will have then—is ours to live now, by faith.

The Spirit that raised Jesus from the dead is active in our lives and in the community of the saints. We can live the resurrection life—that we will have at the end of time—in the present. We can live it individually. We can live it as a community. The resurrection power is the Holy Spirit. He exalts Christ in our eyes so that we will seek to live his life after him.

> *If then you have been raised with Christ, seek the things that are above, where Christ is, seated at the right hand of God. Set your minds on things that are above, not on things that are on earth. For you have died, and your life is hidden with Christ in God. When Christ who is your life appears, then you also will appear with him in glory* (Colossians 3:1–4).

You may as well live resurrection life. There is no other life left anyway. ***Your life is hidden with***

Christ in God. The only life left is the life of Christ, and that is lived by faith. Your future resurrection life breaking into the present is the only life available until Jesus returns.

Therefore, kill the death in your life.

As Paul's letter to the Colossians continues, he addresses two kinds of death, and they are both deaths that live between people. They are both deaths of the Trinitarian image of God in us. The first is death in the sexual relationships of the world (Colossians 3:5-7). The second, which is the one that concerns us, is the death in the way that we treat one another.

> *But now you must put them all away: anger, wrath, malice, slander, and obscene talk from your mouth. Do not lie to one another* (Colossians 3:8–9a).

Paul lists fellowship destroyers: anger (hostile feelings), wrath (acting on anger), malice (ill will), slander (attempts to harm someone's reputation), obscene conversation, and lying. They are out of line with the image of the Trinitarian God. These undo relationships.

We are called, as Christians, to look at Jesus, and then serve him in the way that we treat the people around us. We return to Jesus what he has done for us by serving our neighbors, families, friends, and enemies. The way that God, in Christ, has treated us is a family trait. We have been called into the family of God. Kindness is a trait of our family. That is how members of this family live.

When we were in Adam—before we were adopted into a new family—we were still slaves to death and the old world. But we are no longer children of Adam. We died with Christ, and we were raised with him. Our old humanity, our connection to the old Adam, was killed. "*Seeing that you have put off the old self* [old man/old Adam/old humanity] *with its practices and have put on the new self* [new man/new Adam/new humanity]*, which is being renewed in knowledge after the image of its creator*" (Colossians 3:9b–10).

In your baptism (Colossians 2:12), you were united to the death and resurrection of Jesus. You died to Adam, the old man, and you were raised to the life of the new Adam. The image of the Trinity has been, and is being, renewed and restored in you.

This changes the way we treat one another, but is also changes the kind of community life we will live. Paul explains that we should become a community, *"where there is neither Greek nor Jew, circumcision nor uncircumcision, Barbarian, Scythian, bond nor free: but Christ is all, and in all"* (Colossians 3:11). A community life where there is neither Greek nor Jew, [an imperial distinction of political importance], circumcision nor uncircumcision, [an old world distinction made by the law], Barbarian, Scythian, [a racial and cultural distinction], bond *nor* free [a socio-economic, and political distinction].

These distinctions can be an excuse for our unkindness. The rivalries in the world based on racial, cultural, economic, political, and religious differences convince us that people do not deserve kindness.

All of the old world distinctions in the law, and all of the old world distinctions within religious paganism and imperial politics—all of the old world separations between people—are done away with in Christ. There is only one distinction now, and it is your relation to Jesus. Christ *is* all, and in all

(Colossians 3:11). That is the only distinction that is ultimate.

It is easier to build community around what we are against than what we are for. It is easier to fake peace *vis-á-vis* a common rival that to fight for real fellowship. But we show our true relation to Jesus by putting off anger and rivalry and pursue kindness.

True fellowship is not based on shared aversion. I have seen marriages that are only bearable during a presidential election. Their antipathy is temporarily turned towards whatever idiot is running for office for the opposition. But a truce is not peace. True fellowship is grown in the garden of shared faith, shared hope, and shared devotion.

True fellowship begins in the memory. Remember God's kindness to you. Remember that each person that you meet is made in the image of God. Remember that rivalry is built on the shaky foundation of, "Not Jesus."

God tells us to drop our old life, to leave it all behind, because we are new. We are not that divided, contentious, angry person anymore. We died with

Christ and came back from the dead. You have new life in Jesus. Stop rolling around in the graveyard and pretending to be dead bodies.

The Scriptures teach that we should be rid of the rivalry and love one another. Because Jesus is healing mankind, his cross and resurrection put a monkey wrench into the spokes of our rivalries. All of our rivalries fly head first over the handlebars.

The cross of Christ lifts our eyes off of our rival by lifting our eyes off of how we have been treated. Te cross of Christ also lifts our eyes from our rivalries by focusing our eyes on Jesus, seated on the right hand of God, resurrected after clogging the rivalrous world systems with his own body.

In Colossians 3:8-9 we were instructed to put off community destroying sins. Now we are putting on virtues which are the foundations of the new community. Paul moves from what we are to 'put off,' to what we are to 'put on.'

> *Put on then, as God's chosen ones, holy and beloved, compassionate hearts, kindness, humility, meekness, and patience, bearing with one another and, if one has a*

complaint against another, forgiving each other; as the Lord has forgiven you, so you also must forgive (Colossians 3:12–13).

Because of all that we learned about Jesus as the creator and redeemer of the world, because the world is a different sort of place now that Jesus has died and risen from the dead, because you have died and risen with Christ, put on these attributes. You are *holy and beloved.* Put off the rivalrous spirit. Be compassionate, kind, humble, meek (gentle), and patient.

Paul assumes the reality and presence of sin in the church. He knows that God has not called together a group of cherubs to a snugglefest. God has called together sinners. We need to expect to need to forgive one another.

Paul assumes that people are going to get tangled with one another. But he says that forgiveness should be the assumed way that Christians solve quarrels.

Forgiveness should be normal for Christians because we are disciples of Jesus. Followers of Jesus who want to be like our master. Be glad to be joined to one another, not because you have found people that are not messed up, but because of the way that Jesus treats you even though you are a helpless case.

We should not be surprised by sin. Being a part of the church means being joined to sinners. We should expect to need forgiveness and expect to extend it.

There are only two options in dealing with sin. Bear with it without bitterness, or confront it so that you can forgive it. Even if there is a full on church brawl, we plan to forgive one another because God, in Christ, has forgiven us.

"*And above all these*" Paul writes, *"put on love" (Colossians 3:14a)*. I appreciate the older translation of the Greek word that is translated as love: charity. Above all these put on charity. It communicates that this love is not just an emotion. It is an active seeking the good of others. It is a love that is aggressive rather than responsive. It is a love that considers what is best for others and seeks their good rather than its own.

This self-giving love, this charity, "*binds everything together in perfect harmony*" (Colossians 3:14b). The bond that holds the people of God together is love. Self-giving, seeking the good of others, considering others as more important than yourself, love.

When we sin against one another and will not humble ourselves in repentance and forgiveness, we are attacking the community of God's people. We are being restored to the image of the God who is the community of the Father, Son, and Spirit. As the church is knit together in love, it becomes more and more like God, bound together in love.

Paul warns that false teachers with fake wisdom will come in and try and break up the fellowship of the church with their self-righteous heresies. But that is not the only way that we can be beguiled out of our reward of fellowship in a community that reflects the image of God. A lack of love for one another is as much a threat to the life of the community as any self-righteous heresy.

Instead, the peace that God has within himself should direct us to a peace with one another. *"And let the peace of Christ rule in your hearts, to which indeed you were called in one body. And be thankful"* (Colossians 3:15), We should look at the peace that God has and then imitate it. We should imitate it as individuals and as a community.

It is a good thing that we have been given to one another. That is why Paul finishes his sentence here with, *and be thankful.* In this context, taking the Greek into account, this means that we are <u>to be thankful</u>. We are to say thank you, for the people that God has put in our church. We should not complain about whom God has given to us. Can you imagine the Holy Spirit complaining to the Father about Jesus? Or Jesus complaining about the Father? Of course not. They are thankful for one another. It should be just as unthinkable for you to complain about whom God has given to you. Be thankful. Love one another. Be patient with one another. Forgive one another. The recipe for fellowship.

When we are kind to one another, when we look at the way we have been treated by God in Jesus Christ, and then treat one another that way, then we are living out the image of God that we are created in. We are created so that we can live the life of God after him.

Put off anger and malice and pursue kindness.

Joseph the Shame-bearer

Now the birth of Jesus Christ took place in this way. When his mother Mary had been betrothed to Joseph, before they came together she was found to be with child from the Holy Spirit. And her husband Joseph, being a just man and unwilling to put her to shame, resolved to divorce her quietly (Matthew 1:18–19).

When I began gardening I thought I'd try jalapeños. The little green heat pockets are the central ingredient of my homemade salsa. In my mind I was going to be serving guests my secret-recipe salsa with peppers grown, "right there, in my own back yard."

But there was a problem: 'Fiesta Barbi' sized peppers. I tried more water. I put in fertilizer. I knew they were getting enough sun, (it was California after all). I vigilantly pulled dead leaves. I was stumped.

When the autumn arrived, like an old friend with a wooly scarf and warm mulled cider, it came time to clear the garden boxes. Then I found the problem. The root system of my jalapeño plants had never grown past the first layer of dirt. I had the wrong kind of soil for a garden box and the rootstock had never taken properly. The dirt was too hard for the plant to penetrate. That shallow and cramped root system produced my misshapen peppers.

So often we want to grow in the Lord. We want to be more like Jesus. We want to be kinder to our family and friends, more courageous with the good news, and be filled with peace and joy, but no amount of force, frustration, or self-condemnation seems to be able to get us there. Our shrivelly little peppers refuses to flourish with a cramped root system. No amount of trimming, watering, or sunlight can overcome cramped roots.

In Joseph's response to Mary we see that shame cramps the root system of kindness. We will not ever be able to give ourselves to kindness, to courage, or to joy while holding onto shame. If we are holding ourselves back, afraid that we will be uncovered, then godliness will wrinkle, wilt, and whither.

Let me introduce you to a heresy that the church condemned as in the year 451AD. The Monophysite heresy,[1] also called Eutychianism, taught that Jesus only has a divine nature and not a complete human nature. At the Council of Constantinople in 451AD, the church gathered and declared that the scriptures clearly teach that Jesus had both a complete divine nature and a complete human nature. He was one person, but he had two natures.

Often, when we read the bible, we are functionally monophysites. We ignore many of the human details

---

[1]. Monophysite: a person who holds that in the person of Jesus Christ there is only one nature (wholly divine or only subordinately human), not two.

of the story of Jesus. But Jesus was completely human. If Jesus has a full human nature, like us in every way but without sin (Heb. 2:14-17), then attention to the details of Jesus human life will reveal to us the life of God. Here in Matthew we are introduced to the kind of man that Jesus had for an earthly Father. This is our introduction to the man that raised Jesus. Since we are not monophysites, the way that Jesus was raised is centrally important. The character of his earthly father, Joseph, is going to be central to his ability to accomplish the mission of his Heavenly Father.

We think of this passage from Matthew as part of the Christmas story. We know the basic outline of the story but sometimes the details escape us because the glory of the overall story gets in the way. This little detail—about how the righteousness of Joseph manifests itself—is often skimmed over, but there is a whole world to explore here.

Mary is pregnant with the savior of the world. But she is betrothed to Joseph.

Now the birth of Jesus Christ took place in this way.

> *When his mother Mary had been betrothed to Joseph, before they came together she was found to be with child from the Holy Spirit* (Matthew 1:18).

Joseph, judicious man that he was, does not want to marry a woman who appears to have been unfaithful to him, just after their engagement and just before the wedding. That would be a recipe for fruitlessness. She seems like she is not the kind of woman that he thought. By all appearances not the kind of woman that you want raising your children. But notice what Matthew tells us.

> *And her husband Joseph, <u>being a just man</u> and unwilling to put her to shame, resolved to divorce her <u>quietly</u>* (Matthew 1:19).

He is a righteous man, therefore he did not want to put Mary to shame. Righteousness does not want shame pressed. He was not worried about his own reputation. He was not thinking, "I better protect myself." He was thinking, "How can I protect Mary?" He wanted to make sure that Mary was not put to shame.

Remember, he believed that she had been unfaithful to him. He believed that she had broken her word. Being ignorant of the whole story, he believed she had wronged him. But he did not press for his rights. He wanted justice and mercy to kiss. He loved justice and loved mercy. His concern was not that she got what was coming to her. His concern was that she be protected from the shame that others would heap upon her for her indiscretions. He was righteous and therefore more concerned that Mary be protected from the shame of her unfaithfulness.

Instead of looking for revenge, Joseph willingly took the blame for their failed engagement. He planned to cancel the wedding *without* blaming Mary. He planned to take the disgrace and indignity himself rather than further expose Mary to shame.

This is what righteousness looks like. This is what a good man does.

This was the man that raised Jesus. Joseph's parenting are still guiding Jesus thirty years later when he meets a woman exposed to the public shame of being caught in adultery.

> *Now early in the morning He came again into the temple, and all the people came to Him; and He sat down and taught them. Then the scribes and Pharisees brought to Him a woman caught in adultery. And when they had set her in the midst, they said to Him, 'Teacher, this woman was caught in adultery, in the very act. Now Moses, in the law, commanded us that such should be stoned. But what do You say?' This they said, testing Him, that they might have something of which to accuse Him. But Jesus stooped down and wrote on the ground with His finger, as though He did not hear (John 8:2-6).*

When Jesus leaned down and began writing in the sand, it is quite possible that he was remembering Joseph's story about his own mother having been in this very situation. She was vulnerable to the grindings of the public shame machine, just like Mary had been when Joseph decided to take matters into his own hands and become her protector.

Jesus, just like his earthly father, steps in and protects this woman caught in adultery.

> *So when they continued asking Him, He raised Himself*

up and said to them, 'He who is without sin among you, let him throw a stone at her first.' And again He stooped down and wrote on the ground Then those who heard it, being convicted by their conscience, went out one by one, beginning with the oldest even to the last. And Jesus was left alone, and the woman standing in the midst. When Jesus had raised Himself up and saw no one but the woman, He said to her, 'Woman, where are those accusers of yours? Has no one condemned you?' She said, 'No one, Lord.' And Jesus said to her, 'Neither do I condemn you; go and sin no more.' Then Jesus spoke to them again, saying, 'I am the light of the world. He who follows Me shall not walk in darkness, but have the light of life' (John 8:7–12).

Jesus protects the woman, deflecting the shame, opening himself up to the accusers. The very next thing that we see in John is the pharisees questioning Jesus' parentage and the decision to kill Jesus as soon as they have the chance. The pharisees were ready to crush. Jesus took the woman out of their sights by stepping into them himself.

But Jesus' earthly father was not the only father leading him to take shame rather than use it to control people. Jesus took this woman's shame, throwing himself into the accuser's public shame machine on her behalf. But his heavenly Father was leading him to take the shame of all of his people in all of the world.

God's people were vulnerable to shame. In fact, the whole world was a woman caught in the very act of adultery. God the father led Jesus to the cross to take all of the shame of all the world onto himself, putting shame to death once and for all.

The curse of shame is that we are afraid to be uncovered. We are afraid to have who we are and what we have done uncovered. We know enough about who we truly are that we hide and cover, camouflage and conceal. We establish a distance between who we truly are and what people can see because we are embarrassed and ashamed of the truth.

Before Jesus was nailed to the cross, he was stripped naked.

> *Then the soldiers, when they had crucified Jesus, took His garments and made four parts, to each soldier a part, and also the tunic. Now the tunic was without seam, woven*

> *from the top in one piece. They said therefore among themselves, "Let us not tear it, but cast lots for it, whose it shall be," that the Scripture might be fulfilled which says: "They divided My garments among them, And for My clothing they cast lots." Therefore the soldiers did these things* (John 19:23–24).

Jesus was hung from a cross naked as he took all of our sin, all of the world's curse, and all of our shame onto himself. He was, like Joseph, stepping in and protecting the ones that were vulnerable to shame.

That is us. Each of us is vulnerable. But Jesus stepped in.

> *Christ has redeemed us from the curse of the law, having become a curse for us (for it is written, 'Cursed is everyone who hangs on a tree'), that the blessing of Abraham might come upon the Gentiles in Christ Jesus, that we might receive the promise of the Spirit through faith* (Galatians 3:13–14).

> *For He made Him who knew no sin to be sin for us, that we might become the righteousness of God in Him* (2 Corinthians 5:21).

When someone brings accusation against you, even if that person is you in your own head, answer this way. "Jesus was crucified naked for me. There is no more condemnation, no more shame. I am Christ's and he is mine."

If the response is, "Well then, Jesus sure has low standards for the company he keeps." Then make sure to simply agree. "You have no idea."

Jesus has willingly, and for the joy set before him, opened himself up to public shame and accusation, unbegrudgingly gone through the humiliation of public nudity for the pleasure of your company.

He has swallowed all of your shame. Taken it onto himself on the cross and, when he breathed his last, he killed it. Forever.

Everything from your past, everything that you are ashamed of, Jesus took to the cross and uncovered it completely, for the whole world to see. Then Jesus was raised from the dead, and all of that shame was left in the grave. God looks at you, knows everything, and there is no shaming in his gaze

Shame creates an aroma that is oppressive. When we control those around us with shame, saying things like, "Don't you realize when you do that how it makes me feel? Don't you realize how other people are going to look at you, or me, when you do that?" That shaming and guilt manipulation create an environment of fear. Where shame reigns, people become more concerned with avoiding the pressure that will be applied if they do the wrong thing than they are concerned with doing right. As soon as the pressure is gone, the motivation to do what is right is gone. Shaming, in the long run, will backfire. God never uses it, and neither should we.

Let's be honest for a moment, then. When we look at the story of Joseph and Mary, who would you be in the story? Would you be one of the people that Joseph was worried about? Would you be the neighbor that Joseph knew would have a field day with the news? Would you be the gossip clucking their tongue about the shame?

Or with the woman caught in adultery, would you be one of the people gathered around the woman, justifying your choice of stone by the fact that she brought it upon herself? Or would you be the woman? Believing that every hard and sharp word flung at you, no matter how much it hurt, was deserved because of your shame. Do you put up with abuse from the people that are supposed to love you because you can see how you don't deserve any better? Because God loves you. And Perfect love casts out fear. *"There is no fear in love; but perfect love casts out fear, because fear involves torment. But he who fears has not been made perfect in love. We love Him because He first loved us."* (1 John 4:18–19).

Jesus doesn't condemn you. Jesus doesn't shame you. Jesus is not embarrassed of you. Jesus took your shame. Jesus took your sin. And so the Father doesn't condemn you. And Jesus' words to you are, "I was shamed publicly so that you would no longer be troubled by fear and shame."

Jesus takes our shame so that we can drop it and live without it. You do not need to hold onto it. It is gone. Your feelings of shame no longer line up with reality. It is only the ghost of an echo of a past that is gone.

But we see that, because Christ has taken our shame, it no longer makes any sense for you to shame others. We are safe in God's care. We can live our lives like Joseph, no longer willing to use shame as a weapon against people.

In fact, it is this forgiveness that digs and turns and softens the soil around our roots so that we can begin producing the fruit that God created us to grow. The kindness, peace, patience, and self-control that we have been unable to grow in our lives can only flourish when the kindness of the cross of Christ digs and turns the soil by relieving us of the shame of our past sin.

Covered in Fig Leaves

And Jesus went into Jerusalem and into the temple. So when He had looked around at all things, as the hour was already late, He went out to Bethany with the twelve. Now the next day, when they had come out from Bethany, He was hungry. And seeing from afar a fig tree having leaves, He went to see if perhaps He would find something on it. When He came to it, He found nothing but leaves, for it was not the season for figs. In response Jesus said to it, "Let no one eat fruit from you ever again." And His disciples heard it. So they came to Jerusalem. Then Jesus went into the temple and began to drive out those who bought and sold in the temple, and overturned the tables of the money changers and the seats of those who sold doves (Mark 11:11–15).

There are some weird passages in scripture. Jesus curses a fig tree because he was hungry and there was no figs. Even though it was not the time of year for figs. This is a strange passage.

One famous atheist says that this is the one time that Jesus acts less than a Christian. But Jesus has not just lost his temper. In fact, Mark tells us that it was not the season for figs. He wants to make sure we see the significance.

Teaching ancient literature for years has taught me a number of things that help when reading the Bible. One of the more important has been learning to read visually. Ancient authors expect us to read with our imagination engaged, trying to see the scene. Because they regularly employ visual echos help us understand the characters and story, especially when it comes to prophecy and fulfillment.

When Odysseus is trying to get home he keeps finding himself underneath olive trees. Sometimes wild, sometimes half cultivated, sometimes fully cultivated. But every time he is stuck someplace, he goes and sits under an olive tree. When he finally gets home, it turns out that his bed is carved out of a living olive tree. Odysseus kept sitting under an olive tree to weep because he missed his wife and his own bed. Homer simply gives us the visual echo, trusting that we are smart enough to get it.

Jesus is doing something similar. He is using a visual echo in order to act out a prophecy.

There are two kinds of prophecies, foretelling, and forth-telling. The first is telling the future. The second is defining the present so that we will know how to live. Jesus, the prophet, priest, and king, is acting the prophet when he curses the fig tree.

It begins in the Garden of Eden. There is only one fruit, besides the fruit of the knowledge of good and evil and the fruit from the tree of life that we know was in the Garden of Eden.

Think of the story. Adam was created out of the dust of the earth. God blew a living spirit into his nose. He came to life and looked around amazed. Then God built and planted the Garden of Eden in front of Adam so that he would know a little bit of what he was doing when he took over as head gardener of Eden and, eventually, the rest of the planet.

But there was the one fruit that he was not supposed to eat. On the tree in the center of the garden grew the fruit of the knowledge of good and evil. God told Adam to not eat that fruit, and the day that he ate it he would surely die. He was to guard and garden the Land of Eden and eventually the whole world. But the fruit on that tree was off limits.

Later God created Eve out of Adam's rib to help him on the mission. In order to multiply, fill the earth, and take dominion over it, turning it all into a garden the way that God had shown him, Adam needed help. Eve was perfectly suited for the mission.

Then that old dragon (Rev. 12:9) came skulking. With murder in his heart, he lied to Eve, telling her that she would not die. Adam, who was standing right there with her (Gen. 3:8), who was the one that had told her that she would die if she ate it, said nothing. Eve—deceived by Adam and the Serpent working together—took the fruit and ate.

Adam then took from her hand and ate. Their eyes were opened. They were naked. They were ashamed. They hid in the trees. They took fig leaves down and tried to figure out how to turn them into clothes to cover their shame.

In the cool of the morning, in the safety and shade of the garden, God came walking. Adam and Eve stayed hidden. They did not want to face God after disobeying. They were naked and ashamed. God called them, giving them an opportunity to confess, but they hid *in their fig leaves*.

Adam and Eve stood, dressed in fig leaves but without the fruit. Their attempt to cover themselves in fig leaves rather than confess their sin to God becomes the reoccurring temptation of God's people.

God sent them out of the garden into exile. He was merciful. He did not kill them. Instead, he killed animals in their place and gave them clothes, beginning the sacrificial system by promising that they would surly die and then killing an animal in their place. He also replaced their false covering with a true covering made from the hides of the sacrificial animals.

They tried to hide their shame. They would not trust in their creator's mercy and grace and love. This image echoes throughout history as God's people hide their sin and shame.

When Moses, after forty years in the wilderness, stands on the edge of the promised land, preparing God's people to go in, he says, you are about to go into this land flowing with milk and honey and filled with figs. Then he says, but if you turn to other gods and listen to their word rather than to the word of your God, you will be kicked out of this land.

When Adam and Eve listened to the voice of a competing god they were kicked out of a garden filled with figs. Moses gives them the visual echo as a reminder. "You will have the same fate if you turn away form God's Word and turn to other gods. Remember the fig leaves. You too can be exiled."

When Isaiah comes along, he promises that Israel is going into exile to the Assyrians (Nineveh is the capital of Assyria, so God sent Jonah to Assyria to prepare the way). Isaiah prophesies that thier armies, rulers, and power are all fig leaves.

> *"All the host of heaven shall rot away, and the skies roll up like a scroll. All their host shall fall, as leaves fall from the vine, like leaves falling from the fig tree."* (Isaiah 34:4).

All of these things that you have used to protect yourself from me are like fig leaves. Isaiah already told them if they would confess their sin and ask for forgiveness that God would forgive them. Instead they gather power to protect themselves. They covered themselves in fig leaves.

When Jesus curses a fig tree outside of Jerusalem, directly after visiting the temple, Jesus is ringing the bell of the prophet's visual echo of Eden.

> *And Jesus went into Jerusalem and into the temple. So when He had looked around at all things, as the hour was already late, He went out to Bethany with*

the twelve. Now the next day, when they had come out from Bethany, He was hungry. And seeing from afar a fig tree having leaves, He went to see if perhaps He would find something on it. When He came to it, He found nothing but leaves, for it was not the season for figs. In response Jesus said to it, "Let no one eat fruit from you ever again." And His disciples heard it. So they came to Jerusalem. Then Jesus went into the temple and began to drive out those who bought and sold in the temple, and overturned the tables of the money changers and the seats of those who sold doves (Mark 11:11–15).

The temple was covered in fig leaves but without fruit. They were trying to use the law and the traditions of the Pharisees to cover their shame. They were making fig leaf clothing out of the temple and the law and their traditions. That was not the law nor the temple's design.

The Temple was the place where they could be honest about their sin and guilt and shame. The mercy and faithful grace of God was woven into the wood and stone. The rituals were all reenactments and promises of the lovingkindness and forgiveness of God. It was the place where the whole world could learn to be honest with their wrongdoing. The temple was to train the nations to draw near to God and find him gracious, merciful, and forgiving.

The Israelites had turned the place of greatest intimacy and transparency into a fig leaf factory.

Jesus uses the visual echo of Eden, Moses in the wilderness, and Isaiah and the exile, to show us that the fate of the temple is sealed. When God's people cover themselves in fig leaves they are ejected from the garden. Jesus then goes back to the temple and cleanses it. He sandwiches the cursing of the fig tree between his two visits to the temple.

Later that day, Jesus declares a final curse over the temple.

> *Now learn this parable from the fig tree: When its branch has already become tender and puts forth leaves, you know that summer is near. So you also, when you see all these things, know that it is near—at the doors! Assuredly, I say to you, this generation will by no means pass away till all these things take*

place. Heaven and earth will pass away, but My words will by no means pass away (Matt. 24:32-35).

Within one generation not one stone will be left upon another.

But that does not ultimately solve the problem.

When Adam tried to cover himself with fig leaves, hide behind the trees, shift the blame, and make excuses, he and all of his descendants were ejected from the Garden.

We were born into exile because Adam tried to cover his sin with fig leaves.

We are all faithful sons and daughters of Adam, constantly tempted to blame-shift, hide, and hunt for fig leaves.

Our need goes all of the way down and all of the way back. We need a new Adam. We need someone to take responsibility where the first Adam blamed.

Thus Jesus.

Jesus came to us when we were exiled in the wilderness. He was baptized in order to identify with us. He took responsibility where Adam blamed. Immediately after he was baptized, Jesus went into the wilderness to be tempted. Where Adam was surrounded by tame animals, Jesus was surrounded by wild animals. Where Adam had all of the food that he would ever need, Jesus was hungry after forty days of fasting. Where Adam was tempted with food and failed, Jesus was tempted with food and overcame. Where Adam failed to trust God's Word, Jesus was tempted to not trust God's Word and overcame. Where Adam was tempted to grasp and take authority, Jesus was tempted and overcame.

The rule of the first Adam led to a cursed scarcity. Hunger, rivalry, and warfare became the norm. Jesus began to travel, bringing peace and feeding people. Adam closed the door to meals with God. Jesus restored people to God's table. In fact, every time they ate with Jesus, they were eating with God.

Finally, when Adam discovered sin and realized that he was naked, he was afraid. He hid behind the trees, and covered himself with fig leaves. He did not believe that God could be trusted with his sin. He did not believe that God could be trusted with his shame.

Jesus volunteered to be made a curse for all of the sin of his people. And not for ours only, but also for the sin of the whole world. Because he took all of that sin onto himself, he was stripped naked, just like Adam. But instead of hiding behind a tree, he was nailed to one. Instead of blaming someone else, he had words of forgiveness on his lips, "Father forgive them." Instead of blaming the woman in his life, he makes sure that she will be taken care of. Instead of hiding from God while all of the shame of all of our sins was displayed in him, he says, "Father, into your hands I commit my Spirit."

Adam received his Spirit from God, and should have known that, even in his sin he could trust his spirit into God's hands. But instead he hid, covering his sin, covering shame. He tried to hold back and protect himself from God. But with God was the only safe place for a sinner.

Jesus knew that he could trust God, even when he was dying for the sins of the world. Even under the curse of sin, he knew that he could trust his Father.

We are fig leaf conversion experts, trying to keep God from seeing how deeply ashamed we are about the true state of our soul. We are afraid that our sin and guilt and shame are too much. We are afraid to admit the thoughts and meditations of our hearts to God because we are really, really screwed up.

We are deeply and fundamentally bent by sin. We try to cover our sin and hide our shame. But the good news is, God can handle your sin and shame.

It is a lie that we have to hide from God (as if we really could). God knows you. God knows about the things that you have done and the things that you have thought about doing. God knows about everything that makes you blush. He knows it and *he still loves you*. His grace is sufficient for you.

You can trust yourself into his hands exactly as you are. You can trust him because Jesus died for you. Jesus took all of your sin and guilt and shame onto himself. You do not need to be any different that you are right now to come to God. He will begin changing you right away, but you can come to God exactly as you are.

Drop every fig leaf that you use to keep God at a distance. You are accepted by God. He has been kind. He is kind. He will be kind.

* * *

Enjoy more of Jason Farley's writing in his poetry collections *No One Doubts a Belly Laugh* and *Twenty Wild Decembers: Poems on Time*, or on his Podcast and blog *The Westminster Confession of Funk*.

Jason is also the author of the novella *Robo-Buffer, I am not Human*, and the children's book, *Waiting through Winter*.

* * *

www.ingramcontent.com/pod-product-compliance
Lightning Source LLC
Chambersburg PA
CBHW051650040426
42446CB00009B/1061